First published by Dog Ear Publishing
4010 W. 86th Street, Ste H
Indianapolis, IN 46268
www.dogearpublishing.net

ISBN: 978-145750-138-8

This book is printed on acid-free paper.

Printed in the United States of America

Table of Contents

Preface

The human services field presents with a myriad of challenges for its leaders. The needs of clients have become more and more complex. So, too, have the needs of employees who work at human service agencies. While undergraduate and graduate programs do an adequate job in educating students for what to expect in the field, many enter the field lacking key skills in terms of leading others. Contemporary leadership experts assert that leaders are made and not born. As such, this places a heavy burden on educational programs and human service organizations to train and develop competent leaders. This is also an area where many educational programs and human service agencies fall short.

Human service organizations and educational programs have long focused on training a competent work force. While this focus has been successful in training staff to adequately meet the needs of the clients they serve, it has led to high turnover in staff because of inadequate supervisory training. Moreover, with little to no focus on training competent leadership, agencies often have to go through a trial and error process before they find and retain competent leaders. Unfortunately, the trial and error process to find a competent leader is very costly to the agency and leads to disgruntled workers and underserved clients. This also commonly leads to individuals getting promoted based on longevity and not on the skills they possess. Also, many productive workers get promoted due to their positive work ethic, but fail as supervisors due to the lack of training and developmental support they receive.

Another issue in human services leadership development is that there is a paradigm shift occurring with regards to how agencies are led. The field is no longer dominated by social workers who focus on systemic issues to be an effective leader. Due to the increasing complexity of client issues and difficulty in attaining and sustaining funding, the human services field requires leaders that are not only client focused, but are highly efficient, innovative, organized, and results oriented. The existing human services model of solely focusing on client needs has now been blended with a data and accountability driven business model. Those that are unable to grasp this will have difficulty sustaining, growing and leading an agency in this changing climate.

The *Essential Handbook for Human Service Leaders* was written to address the deficit in leadership development within the human services field. This book was written to provide the first-time supervisor, as well as those with previous management experience, with vital information to be efficient, competent, and successful in motivating and inspiring employees to meet and exceed their professional potentials. Moreover, this book provides the reader with many actionable examples on how to improve in a specific area or competency. We have worked hard to minimize the focus on philosophy and provide as many real examples as possible so that this book can pay immediate dividends.

We firmly believe that the information contained in this book will lead to improved client and employee satisfaction, outcomes, employee well-being and retention. We wish you the best in your journey to becoming effective leaders within the human services field.

Sincerely,

Tim Nolan and Keith Johnson

Introduction

The ability to make a difference in the lives of others is what attracts most people to the human services field. Some enjoy the direct contact with clients while others seek career advancement into the ranks of management. Being in management affords you the opportunity to model, coach, and guide employees to reach peak performance, but is not without its challenges. Effective leaders are able to balance the many responsibilities of their position while ensuring that client and employee needs are met.

There is a level of responsibility charged to you by being in the leadership position that you are in. You will be asked to lead a team of individuals and in the process be held responsible to ensure that they meet specific standards and expectations. This can be a difficult situation for many, as they are not mentally prepared to lead others and hold them accountable. Being a supervisor is not easy, but it can be highly rewarding when employees grow from your feedback and coaching. Ultimately raising the skill level of supervising can be an admiral achievement.

Being an effective leader requires several core skills: self-reflection, vision, accountability, innovation and collaboration, to name a few. It is vital that you are able to assess your own performance on a continuous basis and pinpoint areas where you are excelling, as well as areas that require growth. Your ability for self-reflection is one of the most important factors that will drive your success as a leader within the field. Due to the complex nature of human personality, you will encounter a wide range of scenarios and behaviors which will continually challenge you.

This is why it is important to assess your performance on an ongoing basis.

The commitment toward continuous quality improvement is another important behavioral trait that a leader needs to possess. The field needs individuals who actively work to challenge the status quo. Innovative environments encourage creativity and excellence. Be open to new ideas and actively seek out others, both internally and externally, who can assist you in developing new systems or enhancing existing ones.

Effective leaders hold themselves and their employees accountable on a consistent basis. Work closely with your team to develop weekly, monthly, quarterly, and/or annual goals and then hold team members accountable to meet or exceed them. The human services field is in dire need of leaders who are not afraid to set lofty goals and then meet them. Holding employees accountable for high levels of performance can be tasking, especially for individuals who have become complacent in their positions, however it can be done. Above all, be able to hold yourself accountable and take responsibility when your team does not meet performance expectations. True leaders acknowledge the strengths as well as areas of need for their team.

Your journey to become a successful and respected leader who can balance client, employee, and organizational needs will be a long and evolving one. There will be times when you feel as though you have a good understanding of the demands and responsibilities of the position, while at other times you will be humbled by your inability to solve a simple situation. Your commitment to personal and professional growth will play a large role in your development and your ability to meet and exceed client and employee needs. Above all, never forget the reason why you entered the field in the first place: to improve the lives of others.

Be Client Focused

Within the human services field, embracing client needs is of the utmost priority. Due to the fact that clients will present with a variety of needs, it is foremost that we never forget the respect that all human beings deserve. This may be difficult given that some clients will present with behaviors that are not congruent with societal standards and values. As a human services leader it will be your role to see beyond your own biases and prejudices to assist the client in making positive changes to their lives.

A client-focused approach entails acknowledging what the exact needs of the client are versus what the professional's perception of what the client needs. One can easily fall into the trap of deciding for the client; however, an effective human services leader should be able to see the global perspective of the client's situation. More importantly, leaders should ensure that their staff remain focused on needs of the clients and do not allow negative entities (i.e. poor relationships with co-workers and external community providers, lack of knowledge to assist a client, etc.) to become barriers to exceptional service delivery.

A client focused approach includes:

- Always approach staff and your supervisor from a standpoint of client needs. Even if it has to do with informing your staff they cannot take vacation for a specific week due to coverage issues, you can always frame it from a standpoint that client needs come first and foremost. This type of approach will maximize objectivity in problem solving situations. Moreover, it will be difficult for staff to see you as being unfair if you are always putting the needs of clients first.

- Staff schedules may have to be adjusted due to the needs of clients. There may be times that staff has to work outside of the normal nine to five schedule to ensure that all client needs are met (i.e. conducting home visits, covering community events, etc.). This may encompass having to work later in some instances, while other situations may call for staff to come in later and leave later. Regardless of the situation, having adequate coverage to meet client needs is of the highest priority. Some examples of meeting client needs includes:
  - In child welfare agencies and juvenile justice programs, for example, workers may have to conduct home visits during irregular hours to meet the needs of biological and/or foster parents.
  - Mental health counselors may have to schedule evening appointments to meet the client's schedule.
- The context of all conversations and interactions should always revolve around a pro-client standpoint. Due to the focus always being on the needs of the client, your language should reflect their best interests. For example, if a client involved with developmental disabilities requires an out-of-county placement, one should ask how that placement will impact their ability to have visits and interaction with their family. When in doubt, the rule should be "How does this decision impact the client?"
- As a human services leader, you want to phrase your questions with staff around the needs of the client. Ask yourself and your staff questions like, "Would this decision impact client care positively or negatively?" "Would this decision improve client care?" etc. Model this type of questioning with your staff so they can understand where you are coming from when they approach you with questions.
- The human services leader is exposed to a variety of situations that are not client related (i.e. staff wanting to take time off, staff calling out sick, staff not wanting specific assignments, underperforming staff, etc.). However, all situations impact client care at some level. Your responsibility

will be to impress upon staff to always think about the needs of the clients first. This will help you remain objective when situations arise. This may result in declining a time off request due to a lack of coverage for upcoming court dates, for example.

- New supervisors commonly encounter issues of being staff aligned as opposed to being focused on client care. Being staff aligned means taking the side of staff without realizing that the decision will impact service to the clients. This is especially true for supervisors who have difficulty confronting their staff and elect to regularly take their side rather than seeing the global picture (i.e. providing the best possible care to clients).

- Be mindful to always be respectful of the client's cultural and ethnic diversity as well as yours and your staff's values and biases. Remember, we all have different biases and bring these into the equation when working with clients (i.e. What is your view of a clean home? This can clearly vary depending on your cultural background).

- Take time to explore the viewpoints that you have toward specific cultural backgrounds as well as any biases that you may have. Oftentimes our lack of knowledge about a specific culture will negatively impact the care that we provide the client, so this is an important area. Become a cultural expert with the backgrounds of the families that you most commonly work with. This can be accomplished by researching information about the culture online or through purchasing cultural diversity books that thoroughly cover specific cultural backgrounds. Encourage staff to do their homework on the cultural background of the clients they are working with. The more that they know about their clients, the better they are able to connect with them. Additionally, take time to explore the same issues with your employees and assess if their views positively or negatively impact client care. After assessing their range of cultural knowledge, find ways to support their development in this area.

- Ensure that you and your staff remain mindful of using the therapeutic tool of meeting clients where they are at. For example, child welfare case managers historically struggle with clients who come from cultures that are different from theirs. Some workers may experience a culture shock when having to visit neighborhoods that are economically depressed. Further, it is important that the worker take into account how their own biases may impact the choices that they feel their clients should make (i.e. The parents spending money for food and electricity versus the children having worn clothing. Some may have difficulty accepting this reality.). It is vital that workers take time to understand the cultural background of the clients that they are working with.

- Mental health counselors should recognize the individual needs of the client and focus solely on those when initially working with them. This should encourage the need for genuineness and allow the therapist to focus on what is important for the client, and not what the therapist thinks the client should address.

- At times, you or your staff may not be in agreement with another provider based on a disagreement or personal dislike for them. It is essential to evaluate providers and situations on what is ultimately in the best interest of the client. Do not allow your own judgment, biases, and prejudices to get in the way of what is needed for the client. Effective human service leaders can take a step back from any given situation and objectively assess what is in the best interest of the client and to not let personal biases get in the way. For example, some agencies may have a timeframe to place a client, but this may not allow for appropriate transition and assessment of their needs (i.e. a child being discharged from a juvenile justice program or a mental facility back into the community). It is imperative that all agencies work collaboratively in assessing the needs to ensure that the client will be successful in their new placement in the community.

Client care drives your mission as a human services leader.

Create a Positive Culture

Culture originates from the very top of the organization and filters downward throughout the rest of the agency. Having a positive culture is just one way to help retain key employees and keep morale high during difficult times. Organizational culture is important from the standpoint that it defines the workplace environment, it communicates to employees what is acceptable and what is not, and informally lets employees know what is expected of them. Unfortunately, this is the downfall of many human service organizations. Many organizations have become so focused on outputs and outcomes that they have lost sight of the well being of their employees.

Some agencies possess a negative and punitive culture that stifles creativity, innovation, and encourages the status quo. Agencies that possess a negative and punitive culture do not encourage collaboration (both internally and externally) and increases turnover for staff who have become complacent, frustrated and feel unvalued. Agencies that possess a powerfully positive culture, on the other hand, reflect not only a philosophy different than that of a negative culture, but also encompasses an atmosphere of growth, development, collaboration, innovation, learning, loyalty, and ultimately helps employees reach work fulfillment.

Culture from agency to agency can be drastically different. One agency may frown upon individuals who dress well, while others may frown upon those who leave exactly at 5:00 p.m. every day. It is important to understand what the accepted culture is for your agency and work to create a positive one in your department, and hopefully your organization.

How to define and develop a positive culture within your department:

- Define what the culture is at the agency through what is expected or implied of its employees. This may include, but is not limited to, dress attire, timeliness of reports, manner of escalating critical issues, staff work hours, and freedom of staff to voice concerns and ideas to improve service delivery without fear of retribution.

- Create goals to help establish what a successful culture looks like, which then optimizes performance for the agency. Possible goals include: observing agency-wide collaboration, positive attitude, positive behavior, going above and beyond for clients/staff, and productivity. For example, how should information flow from senior management to middle management to direct line staff? Another example could include how staff members take initiative to assist other departments that are struggling to provide high quality care.

- While you may not be able to change the culture of your agency, you can start with your department. If you have monthly meetings with your team, you can start to discuss your intentions about addressing the culture and attain feedback from staff. Responding to this feedback as to what is going well and what needs to be changed about what they like and what they would like to see improved, can help gain staff buy-in for the department. For example, speaking to staff individually regarding their concerns can create an environment to make staff feel comfortable. This encourages commitment by individual staff to the decisions of management.

- By developing cultural expectations of your department and sharing them with your peers, you can help to infuse these positive ideas throughout the agency. Furthermore, do not neglect to share your ideas with your supervisor at some point so you can hopefully get them to agree to the usefulness of the idea and support it.

Promoting a positive culture means:

- Taking employee satisfaction seriously through using staff feedback to make change. The use of an annual or quarterly anonymous employee survey or suggestion box can help employees freely share their ideas to improve department performance. Act upon and acknowledge feedback from staff, and implement suggestions that you feel would enhance performance within the department.
- Recognizing employees who personify the standards of the department and agency, both formally and informally. This can be accomplished through simple (i.e. making a comment, email, post-it notes, etc.) to more formal (i.e. recognition dinner, employee of the month, or lunch award) recognition.
- Providing the tools that employees need to do their job (i.e. workstation, necessary technology and communication tools, etc.). For example, when a new employee starts it is critical to have all needed tools in place as close to the first day as possible. Additionally, if the agency undergoes reorganization or a physical change, all employees should be provided with the necessary tools within the first day of this change (i.e. having to move office space). New and existing employees may feel as though the agency is not committed to them if they are not provided with the tools to perform their job in a timely manner. This also implies a lack of foresight by the supervisor and the agency if employee needs are not met.
- Taking care of your employees also demonstrates to them that you and the agency are committed to their well-being. For example, if an employee is out on medical leave, personal contact from the immediate supervisor should be frequent (i.e. phone calls, emails, text messages, etc.). Moreover, the supervisor should be empathetic to the concerns and fears that the employee may have in regards to their leave time. Ultimately, the supervisor and the agency should assure the employee that all efforts are being made to accommodate them and their situation within agency guidelines. However, the supervisor and the agency need to

explore all avenues available and share those efforts with the employee.

- Championing events to enhance cohesiveness and camaraderie among staff (i.e. quarterly picnic, bowling, attending a sporting event, dinner, going out for drinks, etc.).
- Utilizing mentors to guide and support new staff as well as existing employees. Mentors should be comprised of individuals who are willing to impart their knowledge and experience freely.
- Positively encouraging staff to address areas of improvement through the use of the "sandwich technique" (i.e. recognizing what staff is doing well followed by the area(s) that they need to address and closing with encouragement of past success). For example, a child welfare supervisor attends a home visit with their staff and observes the interactions of the worker and the foster parent, and/or biological parent. Upon returning to the office, the supervisor would highlight the positive interactions with the client and praise the employee for those behaviors. Then, the supervisor would share with the worker areas that need improvement. Lastly, the supervisor would then point the overall positive efforts of the employee. The benefit of using the sandwich technique is that it allows the supervisor to provide feedback in a manner that will optimize employee performance.
- Communicating to employees that they can make mistakes without fear of punitive measures, which then enables the opportunity for growth and learning to occur. For example, a case manager from a developmental disability agency fails to secure a placement for a client and the supervisor becomes notified of this. First, resolution for the placement needs to occur. Second, a review of the barriers along with the events that led to employee's non-performance. Constructive review and implementation of work processes of the employee to prevent future incidents can help the employee learn from their mistake in a helpful manner. Remember, the role of the supervisor is to help their employees learn and grow.

- Creating a feeling of excitement for individuals to do their job through being energetic in addressing employee accomplishments. Having a high level of energy and actively encouraging employees to be excited about their jobs and their ideas is crucial to your department's growth. Send out emails to the department and agency to celebrate employee accomplishments, post accomplishments on the agency bulletin board, etc.

A positive culture cultivates a learning environment and an atmosphere of success.

Set High Standards

Setting high standards for employees is typically an area of need within the human services field. Setting high standards for yourself and your staff is multifaceted. It can range from ensuring that paperwork is completed on time, reports are submitted early and of high quality, and clinical notes are well written, to staff going above and beyond to ensure that client, funder, and agency/coworker needs are met.

Human service leaders are in a pivotal role to set high standards. Many workers will complain that their case loads are too high or they do not have the resources to adequately meet client needs. However, it is the role of the supervisor to ensure that there are efficient systems and tools in place to support staff so that high standards can be communicated and attained on a consistent basis.

Ways to set high standards for yourself and your staff include:

- Only accept work of the highest quality. If that means that staff has to revise their work several times, it should only take a few instances of this before they appreciate the value of quality work.
- Hold yourself and your staff to a high level and remind staff that the quality of their work not only reflects upon them, but also the agency. For example, submission of documents to the court and other agencies should be of the highest quality, otherwise the credibility of the staff, supervisor, and agency will suffer.

- Reports and emails encompass an integral part of work in the field. Having correct grammar, spelling and content are essential components to writing high quality reports and emails. If staff has difficulty in meeting this standard, it is important to address any potential barriers as well as provide concrete examples of what a high quality report and/or email looks like. Ensure that staff use spell check and write emails in Word before cutting and pasting them into the email if necessary.
- Staff should always be mindful of whom their audience is when writing reports (i.e. judges, Guardian Ad Litems, attorneys, parents, etc.) and their respective level of expertise. Work with staff to address those different levels of expertise when writing reports or emails.
- Setting high standards also centers on how you and your staff address client issues. You want staff that are committed to client needs and can initiate services with minimal prompting from you. Review your standards and expectations regularly with staff, and provide feedback and praise to reinforce high quality client care.
    - For example, if the fundraising department requests information to complete a grant application, staff should forward any requested documentation in a prompt manner. Staff should be mindful of the sense of urgency needed and respond appropriately. Moreover, they should be friendly and accommodating.
    - In a mental health setting, if a former client calls requesting information or referral resources, staff should spend the necessary time to address their needs. Staff should always work to assist individuals whether they are current clients are not.
    - In an organization, staff should assist coworkers and initiate support whenever possible. This helps to foster a sense of collaboration within the department/agency.
- The supervisor has a crucial role in setting high standards within the department. Setting high standards comes down

to the pride that you and your staff model for internal members of the agency and the community at large.

- Integrity is another aspect of high standards. Unfortunately, employees do commit fraud from time to time (i.e. fabricating whether or not they have seen clients, services provided to clients, etc.). Be sure to speak to staff ahead of time and inform them that any breaches in integrity will not be tolerated. It is not worth having your career ruined due to trying to take unnecessary shortcuts.
- Regularly communicate the importance of high standards and how it impacts the reputation of the employee and the agency as a whole. This will help staff to see issues from a more global perspective.

Setting high standards equals superior client care and organizational excellence.

Work with a High Sense of Urgency

The human services field does not often portray a positive image, overall, with regards to approaching tasks and situations with a high sense of urgency. Reasons for this negative perception may include, but are not limited to, the following: overworked and underpaid staff, high staff turnover, and negative organizational cultures. With this being said, it is essential that all workers, regardless of their position, work with a high sense of urgency to complete tasks. When working with clients, especially those involved in the child welfare system, the system often is very slow to attend to client needs. As such, be mindful of this and make sure that deadlines are developed for tasks and staff follows through on these deadlines.

By definition, working with a high sense of urgency means not waiting until later that day or the next day to complete a task for a client, for one of your employees, a provider, or a funder. It means making the phone call right away to follow up on a task that should have been accomplished yesterday. It means emailing out the spreadsheet when you are on the phone with the person that needs it. Working with a high sense of urgency also means scheduling an interview or a meeting with a client or a candidate the same or next day if they can make it.

If your staff encounters any issues with meeting objectives, make sure they are communicating with you ahead of time what the issue(s) are so that you can assist if needed. Clients waiting for services typically do not have any idea what is occurring behind the scenes, so they expect that if someone informs them that a specific referral or service will be initiated at a certain time, they expect for it to happen.

How to ensure that you and your staff effectively set deadlines and work with a high sense of urgency in completing tasks:

- Utilize and become proficient with software such as Microsoft Outlook to schedule and flag tasks for employees to complete. For example, if a treatment plan and/or report are due on a specific date, the supervisor can use Microsoft Outlook to notify the employee in advance that the task needs to be completed by that time.
- After flagging or setting a task for staff, it is vital that the supervisor personally follow up with them on the status of completing the task. This can be accomplished through supervision as well as informal interactions with staff to see how they are progressing with a given task. This allows staff to communicate as well as proactively address barriers that may impede completing the task within the required time-frame.
- Provide staff concrete deadlines for completing work and following through to ensure that it is completed by the scheduled time. For example, if specific information is needed to complete a report to your supervisor by Wednesday, inform your staff that it is needed by Monday at noon. This allows time to review the information, have staff edit it if necessary, or work with staff that is delinquent in providing the information to you in a timely manner.
- Encourage staff to complete tasks before due dates. For example, if a report to the court or a foster home relicensing packet is due on a specific date, have employees submit the documents three days prior. This will enhance the agency's creditability and relationship with external providers (i.e. the court system, funders, etc.).
- Encourage staff to communicate barriers to completing tasks well in advance of due dates. It is counterproductive to find out at the last minute that a specific task will not be completed within a given timeframe. Furthermore, when issues are not communicated ahead of time, it causes undue

stress to all staff involved on a project, as well as negatively impacts client care. For example, if a relicensing packet is not submitted on time for a foster home, it may negatively impact the placement of the children who reside there.

- Model how to increase multitasking abilities with your staff. Some staff can only work on one task at a time; work with them individually on how to complete more than one assignment at a time.
- Be conscious of your most productive period(s) of the day and center the bulk of your work during those times (i.e. just before lunch, early in the morning, etc.).

Accomplishing tasks with a high sense of urgency will do the following:

- The supervisor will gain a high level of credibility if they operate a department where there is a clear expectation for staff to accomplish tasks with a high sense of urgency. This is a competency that will quickly allow the department and agency to stand out.
- Staff will work more efficiently in completing tasks if they are able to work more efficiently when needed. This will allow productivity to increase and leave staff with more time to address other client-related issues.
- Client care and client satisfaction will also improve given that needed services and referrals are made within a timely manner.
- Departments that work with a high sense of urgency will experience decreased levels of stress and will also create an optimal environment for efficiency.

Cultivating a high sense of urgency will enhance the department/organization's credibility and lead to exceptional client care.

Deliver on Commitments and Following Through

Delivering on commitments and following through is an area that the human services field consistently struggles with. Tasks that are not completed within a timely manner and/or commitments not kept weakens credibility. Following through may range from stating that a referral will be made by a certain date, a service will begin by a specified date, or a specific person will be contacted by a specific timeframe. Think of a time in which you attended a meeting and specific tasks were to be followed up on only to find out that they were not. Whenever human service professionals do not follow through, the clients ultimately suffer the consequences.

Promptly following through on tasks and keeping commitments goes a long way to ensuring that high quality client care is provided, as well as building credibility for the supervisors and the agency. Many will argue that it is very difficult to keep track of all obligations and commitments due to high case loads or high client demands. There are many workers that find a way to balance all responsibilities and tasks. High performance organizations are comprised of many employees who consistently and effectively multitask to meet client needs.

Key points in regard to keeping commitments and following through:

- As a human services leader it is easy to get overcommitted because of the desire to help. As such, be mindful to deliver on all commitments that you make and deliver early if possible. Also, one needs to be cognizant of their workload so that they do not become overextended.

- For example, workers may become frustrated at times when they assume responsibilities outside of their job duties. The role of the supervisor is to help the worker focus on department/agency priorities. Workers who go above and beyond to assist others must also recognize balance.

- You will gain a great deal of credibility, both internally within your organization and externally with outside providers, if you consistently deliver on commitments that you make. It is frustrating when a supervisor makes commitments, but consistently does not deliver on what they say. Be mindful of this and be sure that you are not that person.

- If you are going to commit to completing a task, be sure to deliver when you say you will or provide an explanation to them as to why you were not able to deliver within the specified timeframe. Providing this explanation when tasks are not completed on time will help you maintain credibility with your staff and clients, as opposed to disappointing or ignoring them. Ongoing communication is crucial, so keep individuals and your supervisor informed throughout the process.

  - For example, if a Case Manager is working to secure a housing voucher/assistance they should maintain constant communication with the client to keep them updated on the process. If it is a high profile situation, keep your supervisor informed of any pertinent activities on the case.

- Ultimately, think of the golden rule when keeping commitments and following through: treat others how you would like to be treated. Furthermore, act quickly and efficiently to follow up on items and ensure that they are completed with a high degree of quality.

- Anytime you or your staff does not follow through for a client, the client is negatively impacted.

- For example, if a Case Manager does not complete necessary referrals on time, it may delay needed services for the family or reunification for the child(ren).

Hold staff accountable for their actions as well as yourself:

- If an employee has a deadline to provide information to you by 5:00 p.m. on Tuesday and it is not received until Wednesday at 10:00 a.m., it is important to process with the employee what barriers they encountered that led to the task not being completed on time. Workers may not see the relevance of the effect of slight tardiness in completing a task on time; however, accountability must be consistently enforced if you are to be a successful human services leader.
- Moreover, staff should be well aware of your expectations for work to be completed within specified timeframes. This is something that should be part of the expectation agreement that you provide them. Regular review of department and individual expectations are important for quality.
- Hold yourself accountable to deliver on commitments. It is important to be congruent and model the behaviors that you expect from staff. If you consistently do not follow through on commitments it will be difficult to ask staff to do the same.

Recommendations on how to ensure you and your staff are delivering on commitments include:

- Keep a notepad of tasks that need to be followed up on and cross them off as they are completed.
- Use a program like Microsoft Outlook to add tasks, due dates, as well as list due items in your calendar and give yourself a reminder of at least one day to ensure you can have it completed.
- Use a calendar to keep track of all appointments and due dates. Set reminders to keep you informed of when tasks are due.
- Use a smart phone (i.e. a Blackberry) that will allow you to have work emails and your calendar synched to your phone.

This will allow you to quickly and efficiently keep track of all work and tasks even if you are not at your desk.

Be Organized

Organization is another important aspect to keeping commitments and following through on tasks. Being organized allows more tasks to be completed with a higher degree of quality. With today's ever evolving technology and access to information, organization equals efficiency. Possessing the ability to multitask will enhance one's ability to stay organized.

Examples on how to increase organization:

- Use of Microsoft Outlook to plan your week, set tasks and due dates for your staff, invite staff to meetings, set reoccurring meetings for yourself and staff that will automatically pop up ahead of time, etc.
- Organize your emails on Microsoft Outlook. You can set up additional folders under the Inbox and Sent folders. For example, you can set up HR, follow up, and intake folders where emails can be easily transferred so they are easy to find and keep track of.
- Use of a day timer to keep track of appointments, due dates, etc.
- Writing lists of tasks and crossing them off as they are completed.

Ways to increase organization for your staff:

- Have staff post their schedule for the week in Microsoft Outlook, use a dry erase board where all department staff write down their schedules for the week, or develop a spreadsheet where all staff can add their schedules for the week so you know how they have their week planned.
- Keep folders and files neatly organized on your computer so you can access them quickly. If you set up categories, it will make it easier for you to store and access needed files. Additionally, if your agency has a shared drive, ensure that all client information is stored on the shared drive and not

on staff computers. This will prove especially helpful if staff is out or a staff member has recently left the agency.

- For example, setting up on the shared agency drive a contact folder that lists all points of contact, phone numbers, and email addresses. This should be categorized by groups (i.e. therapy providers, residential providers, etc.).

A quality reputation is built through organization, consistency, and quality.

Personalizing Your Approach

Many of the core skills and techniques that are used in working with clients can also be utilized in your relationship with your staff. Skills such as empathy, inspiration to excel, reflective listening, and working from a strength-based approach can be used with your staff. Too often, we forget why we choose to work in the human services field and do not use the valuable aforementioned skills with our staff. As such, your personalized approach with your staff is vital to being successful.

Research shows that individuals are more likely to stay with an organization if they have a supportive relationship with their supervisor. For example, in child welfare organizations most workers are inexperienced, and subsequently this may impact turnover rates. The inexperience of workers interacting with biological parents, and with the child welfare system in general, is an area that the supervisor needs to pay close attention to (i.e. helping to adequately prepare and support workers when working with difficult parents and/or clients). Turnover rates of child welfare case workers have a negative effect on permanency for children. As such, supervisors need to closely support, mentor, and guide new workers so that they can meet client needs and experience individual satisfaction as well as professional competence.

Take time to sit down and define your approach. What is important to you as a supervisor? How do you want others to perceive you? By clearly defining your approach and how you intend to attain peak performance from your staff, you can maximize their performance.

Your goal is to be the supervisor that staff feels comfortable coming to. Hopefully, your staff will approach you across all situations, including: if they experience any barriers in working with clients, make a mistake and need guidance, have suggestions to improve service delivery, or have a personal issue that impedes their work performance. Additionally, you want to be the supervisor who inspires your staff to reach new heights and work in an environment that promotes learning and growth.

How to personalize your approach with staff:

- Present to your staff that you have an open door policy. Encourage them to informally stop by and discuss any issues that they may be having or provide ideas on how to improve existing systems.
- Be open to feedback from staff regarding your approach and allow staff to provide feedback to you. Even though you may not agree with what they have to say, they may end up providing you with helpful feedback to improve your performance. Also, staff feedback can bring attention to an aspect of your approach that you were previously unaware of. Be congruent with your staff by demonstrating body language, word choice, and tone that is open and receptive to the feedback that you receive. Take time to thank staff for sharing their feedback.
- Encourage staff to offer different viewpoints. The more viewpoints on an issue the better, as long as it is in a professional and respectable manner. For example, several staff members are discussing treatment options for a client; staff is discussing how to respond to a concern from a funder, etc. This is going to take some work, but you want staff to also trust that if they openly disagree on an issue there will be no retribution from you. Model and provide examples to your staff of what a professional dialogue looks like (i.e. how to offer and clarify different viewpoints objectively, how to disagree in a professional manner, etc.).
  - Utilizing proper word choice when involved in dialogue with others is important to getting your viewpoint across. For example, if one wants to advocate

for a particular position, proper word choice may include: "What options are we considering?" versus "We need to make a decision."

- Provide continuous feedback to your staff. Staff needs to know that you are paying attention and are observant of their activities. Make a concerted effort to catch your staff doing well. This will help to create balance and objectivity when you provide your staff with constructive criticism.

- Make an effort to check in with staff on a periodic basis in an informal manner and see how they are doing. Acknowledging staff when you arrive in the morning or leave in the evening is an excellent time to do this. This will help you present as more approachable and sincere. Remember, it is important to use the skills that you have been taught for clients and use them with staff. The more approachable you are to staff, the more information will flow your way.

- Take time to find out something personal about your staff and use it as a conversational tool for future discussions (i.e. names of their children, favorite television shows, favorite sports teams, etc.).

- Spend time with staff. Staff appreciates when supervisors take time to get to know them on a personal level rather than relying on what others say about them. Additionally, take time to fully understand their job duties so that you have first-hand knowledge of what they do on a daily basis. Employees typically complain that their supervisors do not know enough about them and the tasks that they perform on a daily basis. The more you know about your staff the more credibility and rapport you will have with them.

- Do not be afraid to reveal a little about yourself. Let staff know some of your favorite sports teams, television shows, or events that you did with your family over the weekend. It goes a long way when staff sees you as a human being and gets to know you a little outside of work.

- While your goal is to have a close relationship and be seen as approachable to your staff, be cognizant to maintain proper boundaries between you and your staff. If staff does not fully respect you and your position, it will undermine your ability as a leader.

- Share information, updates on agency issues, and developments within the field with staff as they become available to you, do not hide them. This can be done during staff meetings or during periodic emails sent to your staff. This will help to create an environment where staff freely seeks out your knowledge and experience. Additionally, this type of environment will help to provide more efficient and knowledgeable staff. Staff should not be excluded regarding agency updates.
- Share your insights and past experiences with your staff. This may include how to approach specific individuals and/or situations. Do not be afraid to share your wisdom with staff. Coaching is a large portion to being a supervisor.
    - For example, if there was a situation in which you really worked hard on but the outcome was different than what you were expecting, share with staff your feelings of disappointment and frustration. This will help to provide perspective.
- Be technically proficient in all areas related to your position. This includes being knowledgeable of all applicable policies and procedures, state statues, federal guidelines, etc. While being an expert is not necessary, the more knowledge that you possess the more competent staff will see you.
- Deliver bad news personally. For example, if an internal candidate applies for a position and is not offered the job, go to them directly to relay the news. Moreover, this will allow you to provide the employee with vital feedback that will promote their growth and development.
- If you have received an internal promotion to a supervisory position, be aware of the challenges ahead of you. It will be important to clearly establish your supervisory position in regards to staff who were formerly your peers. Employees who were former peers may be slow to respect your new position and may expect preferential treatment. It is crucial to be aware of this and to reinforce your expectations and position differential with staff. Consider the implementation of unit/team goals to help everyone focus on a shared purpose.

Be Self-Reflective

- One of the key ingredients to being a successful leader is the ability to be self-reflective. Being self-reflective allows you to look at situations and be open to how they could have been handled differently, and then using this new-found knowledge in the future. Regularly evaluate your performance and give yourself feedback on how you are doing. Never become complacent; continually strive to achieve higher goals for yourself, your staff, and the clients that you serve.

- Always be mindful of your role in the negative or positive outcomes of situations. Being self-reflective allows you to carefully examine your role in why a situation was successful (i.e. a meeting to determine placement for a child) or why it was not (i.e. a decision to promote an individual without performing adequate research on their job performance). Encourage your employees to take on this approach as well.

- Examples of being self-reflective include: reviewing your performance during a meeting and how you could have communicated a specific message differently, reviewing your performance during a supervision session with an employee and how you could have better addressed a needed area of improvement for them, etc.

- Keep a journal or taking notes is an excellent way to evaluate situations and monitor how you are progressing with a specific competency. For example, you could monitor how well you are doing providing feedback to employees and track your progress with your journal. This is an excellent tool to share with a mentor or your supervisor for additional support and feedback.

- Additionally, being self-reflective is a skill that you want to model for staff. Sharing some of your thought process with staff and how you approach specific situations can be very useful to helping staff with their growth. Examples include: retracing an event, pointing out a missed cue, etc.

- Be self-reflective when having supervision with your supervisor. Again, the idea is to grow and the only way to do that is to be mindful of your approach and thought process. Openly share areas that you are struggling with and do not be afraid to ask for support and guidance.

- Do not be afraid to admit mistakes to your staff. If an event arises in which you feel that you could have handled it differently, try to take advantage of the 24 hour window of opportunity and debrief the situation with your staff. This will demonstrate to your staff that you, too, make mistakes and can take accountability for the mistakes that have been made. Additionally, this will help to improve your relationship with staff as well as your credibility as a human services leader.

Work/Life Balance

This is an area that many new supervisors struggle with. While many supervisory positions require extra time beyond the standard work week, having balance between your personal and professional lives is essential. Demonstrating a work/life balance will help model the same approach to your staff. Ultimately, if you do not have balance between your professional and personal life, your job performance will suffer.

Ways to achieve a work/life balance:

- A typical human services supervisor works as much as 45-50 hours a week. Be mindful of this and if your schedule exceeds this threshold, assess and re-evaluate your approach and responsibilities. For example, delegating more to your staff, and asking other peers to handle any shared agency responsibilities such as chairing committees, etc.
- Taking vacation days are imperative to recharging. Regardless of how many responsibilities you have, you need to make time for yourself. Additionally, when taking time off it is essential to totally disconnect from work (i.e. turn off your agency cell phone, do not check email, do not call and check in with your staff, do not take work with you, etc.).
- Limit the amount of work that you take home with you. This should only be done occasionally.

- Utilize stress reducing techniques (i.e. working out, listening to music, walking on the beach, engaging in hobbies, etc.).

Identify your personal approach strengths and how effective they can be in dealing with others.

Conflict Resolution and Feedback

Conflict is natural and healthy. In fact, conflict can be an asset to the department and/or agency if handled correctly. Departments and agencies need individuals who bring their own opinions and perspectives, as this only helps to improve client care and organizational efficiency. Individuals have their own style for handling conflict, and it is important to recognize what that is and how it affects their ability to hold their staff accountable.

However, if you have difficulty with conflict providing feedback will be a challenge. Be cognizant of your comfort level with regards to handling conflict and what your approach is to addressing conflict. Few, if any, supervisors look forward to providing constructive feedback to employees, but it is necessary. Moreover, when employees sense that you are reluctant to address issues it will negatively impact your credibility and ability to hold them accountable.

The conflict resolution continuum

- Thomas-Kilmann identified five main styles to approaching and resolving conflict. Take a moment to assess where you think you are and how that may impact your ability to lead your team:
    - Avoiders: This involves individuals who may deny that an issue exists. There may be times that they are aware of an issue being present, but attempt to avert or ignore the conflict. They may find conflict anxiety provoking and seek to avoid it at all costs. For example, an employee may consistently be tardy to

work, but the supervisor avoids the issue despite being aware of it.

- Accommodators: Individuals are typically more concerned with the needs of others than themselves. Supervisors who fall in this category may go out of their way to take care of their employees. Be cognizant that being too staff aligned may result in too many concessions being made and lead to reduced managerial credibility. For example, a supervisor may consistently take on the work of their employees to help be a team player despite their own responsibilities.

- Competitors: Individuals who fall into this category constantly compete and may be considered aggressive by their peers and/or employees, and typically put in great effort to be right. Competitors can be assertive given the right circumstance. For example, a peer provides feedback to a supervisor based on an observation that they have and the supervisor immediately begins to point out the negative attributes of the peer or their department.

- Compromisers: These are individuals who fall in the middle of the continuum. The process of obtaining a compromise means that in some instances a win-win solution is not obtained. For example, the supervisor identifies a solution for how individuals will take vacations, but not everyone is satisfied.

- Collaborators: This group is comprised of individuals who encourage everyone to be involved in solving problems. Supervisors who use this type of conflict resolution style engage in a variety of strategies where all parties are actively engaged and involved in the decision-making process. For example, if staff members are having an issue with how a policy and procedure affects them and their ability to complete their job responsibilities, the supervisor has all staff get together, discuss the issues, and arrive at a mutual solution.

The benefits and challenges of addressing conflict

- Conflict naturally occurs in the workplace. It is important to realize this and to proactively address situations where conflicts arise. For example, if staff is unhappy with a management decision, move decisively to address this. You can have an all-staff meeting to address the concerns or you can meet with staff individually to find the root of their discontent.

- While few may fall into any of the categories that Thomas-Kilmann describes, it is important to recognize how your approach to conflict may be helping or hurting your ability to engage your employees. Those that avoid conflict may be less likely to provide accurate performance feedback to staff. Conversely, those that cannot accept feedback (competitors) may have difficulty connecting with their employees due to not embracing opportunities for improvement.

- Supervisors that avoid addressing conflict risk losing credibility and control of their departments. For example, if an employee does not receive a promotion and then becomes a negative influence on the rest of the department, it is imperative that the supervisor quickly meet with the employee individually to address the reasons for their discontent. Moreover, this is a good opportunity for the supervisor to provide coaching to the employee to assist them with improving their professional maturity.

- Be attentive to the overall mood in your department. Check in with staff frequently to keep your pulse on the unit. Many times there is at least one employee that will serve as an unofficial liaison and help you stay connected, take advantage of this.

- Take advantage of opportunities to assess the stress levels of your team, both individually and as a group. When individuals experience high levels of stress, conflict is more likely. There are times that you can help and pitch in to reduce the stress levels of your employees.

- Review with your supervisor, a peer, or a representative from the human resources department on how to address conflict. Role play situations that you may have to address to help increase your comfort level.

- Addressing conflict is never easy and typically causes anxiety, but experienced leaders know the value in proactively addressing individuals and situations before they become worse. Think of conflict as an opportunity to model leadership for your employees.

Strong and decisive leaders proactively address conflict.

Engaging Difficult Employees

Difficult employees can appear in all departments and organizations. The reason why employees are considered hard to work with are many, however your role will be to challenge them to maximize their professional potentials. Be mindful of how your approach to conflict can assist or impede your efforts to turn around negative behavior.

There are a variety of reasons why an individual has disconnected from their work environment and your role is to find out why. There are times when it is truly not the employee's fault. They may have worked in environments that were hostile, did not embrace creativity, or recognize achievement. Still, your ability to engage and help a problem employee turn into an active contributor to the department and agency will be a crowning achievement in your career.

What constitutes a difficult employee:
- Negative/poor attitude
- Frequent questioning and/or challenging of management decisions
- Problems getting along with peers
- Difficulty engaging clients
- Struggles to be a team player
- Insubordinate
- Unmotivated to do more than bare minimum
- Poor or inconsistent work performance

Reasons why employees are considered difficult:

- Burned out
- Complacent-they have been in the position for a long period of time
- Personal dissatisfaction (i.e. personal issues outside of the workplace)
- Professional dissatisfaction (e.g. they have lost out on prior promotional opportunities, been demoted, feel their ideas have not been considered and/or implemented, etc.)
- Difficult personalities

Ways to address employees who are considered difficult:

- Seek to form a relationship with all employees, especially those that are considered difficult. While it may be a challenge to do this, go out of your way to create opportunities to engage them throughout the day. Consider it a project and spend a little extra time with the individual. One of the reasons why they may have disconnected is that they feel no one has taken an interest in them. There are times when simply taking an interest in the person may go a long way to turning things around.
- Spend time with the employee so that you can form an opinion on them first hand. Sometimes individuals get a negative reputation and this can cause others to judge them. Take time to find out about the employee and make your own assessment; there are times when what we experience firsthand may not coincide with what you hear.
- Create opportunities to empower the individual. Even though it may be easier to point out their negative attributes, find at least one positive attribute and build from there. For example, if an employee is very competent but has a negative attitude, empower them to train others or take the lead on specific projects.
- Ask for feedback. Do not hesitate to involve the employee in decisions and see if this can help to energize them. If an employee is burned out they may flourish under different conditions and with new opportunities. This is also why it can be a good idea to work with the human resources

department to see if a transfer would benefit the employee; sometimes a change in scenery can be helpful.

- Build trust. Some employees do not trust management and this can be a major factor in their lack of engagement with the organization. Be as transparent as possible, when appropriate, and keep staff informed of agency changes, developments, and news.

- Find ways to motivate and inspire. For employees that are burned out they have lost the connection to why they have entered the field. Help them to reconnect with how it feels to help others (clients and colleagues) and use this as a foundation to engage them. We all need reminders from time to time of why we chose to enter the helping profession.

- Provide positive reinforcement. Take time to point out the positive behaviors that the employee demonstrates. If they are considered a difficult employee it will be easy to point out the negative aspects of their performance, but resist this urge. Make an effort to point out at least 2-3 positive behaviors per day (i.e. "Nice job following up on that request"; "I liked how you positively responded to that difficult client," etc.). Be mindful to be specific in your praise and to be genuine.

- Process with the employee your perception of their difficult nature and obtain their feedback. Be direct, yet gentle, with employees who are having difficulty buying into the culture of the organization of struggling to meet expectations. By having frank conversations you can assess the reasons for their discontent and evaluate if they are legitimate or not. Be receptive to the feedback that they provide and be able to accept responsibility for why the employee is not maximizing their potential. Human behavior is complex and so too are the reasons why individuals disengage from their work environments.

- For individuals who have previously applied for promotional opportunities and have not received them, work with the employee to expand their skill sets. Take time to review what they have applied for and obtain feedback from internal and external stakeholders and provide specific training to help them grow and develop. Demonstrate your commitment to staff and this will usually be rewarded in increased effort and improved morale. Schedule extra time to meet with staff or expand regularly held supervision meetings to focus on areas of development.

- If the employee is having performance issues, take time to carefully review expectations and provide guidance on how they can achieve those expectations. Supervisors sometimes waiver between wanting to quickly pursue disciplinary action for underperforming employees to not actively holding them accountable. Understand that some individuals take longer to adjust to tasks or work at a different pace than others. See how you can best utilize the individual skills of the employee to benefit the department and clients that you serve.

- Despite all efforts some employees may not have the insight or the desire to turn around their behavior. If that is the case, consult with your supervisor and the human resources department on how to move forward. There are times when progressive disciplinary action is necessary to turn around behavior or to remove the individual from the department and organization. This should be a last resort, however.

Work closely with difficult staff to maximize their professional potentials.

Dress and Act Professionally

Professionalism is one of the core traits to being a successful leader in the human services field. Important components to being professional include appropriate attire and behavior. Consistently dressing and acting professionally communicates to clients, staff, and members of the community that you have a "make it happen" personality and possess the integrity to meet client needs.

With regards to professional attire, it makes a strong statement when supervisors present in attire that is considered professional. Professional attire demonstrates to other human service professionals and clients that you are committed to providing exceptional services. Different levels of professional attire are dependent on the demands of the activity.

Being aware of how you speak and respond (both verbally and nonverbally) are important aspects of behaving professionally. Furthermore, it is important to consider that your behaviors are always being observed by your staff, other members of your organization, and the community. As such, it is important to portray professionalism at all times.

Important aspects of professional attire:
- Presenting in a professional manner, both in behavior and dress, is just one of many ways to help you gain credibility, as first impressions are very important.
- Recommended professional attire for men includes slacks, dress shirt, a tie, and appropriate footwear. One's level of attire should be consistent with the activity they are

engaging in (i.e. wearing a shirt and tie to a meeting, but dressing in business casual if meeting with clients).

- Recommended professional attire for women includes dress pants, appropriate skirt, dress shirt, and footwear. Again, one's level of attire should be consistent with the activity that is being engaged in.
- By presenting with a professional look you are modeling for your staff appropriate levels of dress attire. Aim to be the best dressed individual in your agency; this will help to set a high standard.
- Dress in business professional attire for any meetings, court hearings, etc.
- Address with staff if they do not meet professional attire expectations.

In regards to professional behavior:

- Addressing situations in a calm and deliberate way is a key ingredient for a human services supervisor. Oftentimes, situations (client and staff related) will arise and others may look for an immediate response from you. By being deliberate and calm in your demeanor, you allow yourself to not act out of emotion when addressing the various issues that will arise. This also relates to any email communications, letters, and memos as well, as you do not want to respond in a way that displays an emotional reaction (it is advisable to read over your response before sending it to ensure that it portrays an objective message and assess how it will be received by others).
- Avoid the pitfall of making an impulsive versus a thoughtful decision. This will allow you to consult with your supervisor, speak to staff to collect more information, consult with a peer, etc. Moreover, it will afford you valuable time to thoroughly review all available options before making a well-thought-out decision. Again, this will save you or your supervisor from having to reverse a decision, which then leads to reduced credibility as a leader. Also, be conscious to not delay making decisions (i.e. waiting two weeks to address an issue that should have been handled in a few

days), as inaction will reduce your credibility with clients and staff. Lastly, some individuals merely ignore issues and hope that they will resolve themselves; a true leader engages these types of situations. Consult with your peers and supervisor if you are uncomfortable or do not know how to address a specific issue.

- Present in a confident manner and inform individuals that you are responsive and will promptly address any issues that come to your attention. Individuals like to be put at ease that their supervisor can deal with situations, regardless of the circumstances. If you encounter an issue that you are not able to resolve on your own, it is acceptable to inform others that you will consult with your supervisor or other personnel, and get them an answer promptly. This shows your commitment to attaining the answer.

- Speak with confidence. Individuals that project a confident speaking style will garner attention and be able to concisely focus on the main points. Moreover, confident speakers can vary their volume and accurately portray visual images to their staff. It is important to speak clearly so that others can understand you.

- Choose your words carefully. Effective human service leaders do not have to overpower/dominate those that they are around and tend to speak less often than others. While it may be tempting to speak out, this allows your words to have more value. Listen to fully understand what others are stating before responding to them.

- If you encounter personal and/or professional struggles and challenges, be aware to not allow this to affect the leadership of the department. A common mistake supervisors can make is displaying anger and/or frustration with their staff because of criticism that they receive from their supervisor. Always be positive and convey a "can do" attitude. If you allow your emotions and/or frustrations to get the best of you it will affect your staff and their performance.

- Be sure that any frustrations you have are only communicated at your level (i.e. other supervisors) and above. Never voice your frustrations about the agency to your staff.

While it may be tempting to want to talk to your staff about events or share agency gossip, this will undermine your credibility as a leader.

- The same goes for choosing to pursue disciplinary actions for staff, discuss the situation with a peer, your supervisor and the human resources department to get an impartial perspective before moving forward. Staff should not be privy to confidential information.

- Use diplomacy whenever possible. As a leader, you are expected to mediate situations of conflict. Do not let your personal views obscure your professional objectivity. This does not mean you cannot provide direct feedback to staff, but always consider how your choice of words, as well as how information is delivered and received by them.

- Professional maturity is a skill that, for some, takes time to develop. Professional maturity is the ability to handle situations, especially if they are not the outcome that you desire (i.e. the candidate you selected is not chosen for the position; your supervisor makes a decision that you do not agree with, etc.). There will be times when decisions are made that go against your viewpoints and the ability to demonstrate your maturity with this is important. If you do not feel comfortable working on this skill with your supervisor, seek out a member of the HR team to assist.

Professional presentation and behavior is essential to leading others.

Hiring and Orienting Quality Employees

The average tenure for human service professionals, especially child welfare and child protective services, is approximately a year and a half. As such, it is imperative to hire and orient quality staff. Moreover, constant turnover is detrimental to client care and agency continuity. By reducing turnover in child welfare, for example, permanency will be achieved sooner. In a juvenile justice setting, reduced turnover will result in clients experiencing shorter periods of probation. Mental health settings will see improved treatment outcomes if therapists remain with the agency for extended periods of time.

As a human services leader, you are responsible to provide the necessary support so staff can excel at their position and achieve individual and professional fulfillment. If not, you will experience high turnover in your department and this will negatively impact staff morale and client care. Specific skill sets are needed to successfully hire and orient quality staff, subsequently prolonging employee longevity. Quality orientation involves more than reviewing policies and procedures and job descriptions; it encompasses a total approach to ensure that new staff is successful.

Navigating the interview process:
- Start by giving a brief historical summary about the agency, philosophy and mission.
- Provide a fact sheet detailing specific information about your department and what is expected of the position

through email, if possible, before the interview. This will afford the candidate the opportunity to think of questions ahead of time and ask them during the interview.

- Use a combination of behavioral based interview questions as well as questions designed to highlight previous experience and strengths of the candidate. Examples of behavioral based interviewing includes: asking candidates specific questions geared toward eliciting responses that fit the behavioral characteristics that you are looking for (i.e. ask questions about a time the candidate has gone above and beyond for a client, about a time they encountered a deadline and had trouble meeting it, about a time they had a client that was hard to engage and how they handled it, about a time they assisted a co-worker, etc.). The use of behavioral based interview questions will help to bring in employees who will meet and exceed department and agency standards.

- Review expectations that the agency will have for the candidate as well as what you, the hiring supervisor, will have for them.

- Consider using assessments to find the right match for the department and/or supervisor. For example, using the Myers-Briggs Type Indicator. This is a good psychometric tool to measure how individuals view the world and make decisions. There are times that regardless of how competent the candidate is they may not be a good match for the position. Assessments can help match the best candidate with the best opportunity.

- Move promptly to advertise, interview and hire if you find the right candidate. Delays in this process may cause you to lose a quality candidate (i.e. not scheduling interviews until a week or later after the closing date). Quality applicants will secure a position elsewhere because of their skill set and attributes, so do not delay. However, during difficult economic times, agencies may have more time to recruit and select candidates. This is the time in which careful review of candidates should occur. Do not hesitate to have second and third interviews to select the right candidate.

- If you do not have the right individual for the position, do not feel that you have to hire someone immediately. Many organizations rush to hire staff to fill vacancies out of desperation. Rushing to fill a vacancy with the wrong candidate will postpone your ability to add an effective member to your team. It is often worth the wait to keep the position open, even if you and your team have to take on extra work in the meantime. Hiring the right person is well worth the wait. Turnover costs the agency valuable time, money, and resources.

A detailed orientation schedule should look like:

- A walk through the agency to introduce the new staff to all employees. This will provide the opportunity for your new staff to form relationships and for the staff to assimilate to the culture of the agency. If your agency is large, it may be beneficial to do this on more than one occasion to help them thoroughly process all of the new information they are receiving.
- Ideally, it would be optimal for your new employee to spend the day visiting and orientating to each department. This will help to increase their understanding of how each department operates and allow them to build positive relationships with internal members of the organization. Moreover, this type of bond will help the employee problem solve situations more efficiently.
- A historical overview and evolution of the agency.
- A detailed orientation of the general philosophies and mission of the agency.
- An overview of the different departments that comprise the agency and the need for interaction and collaboration between all such departments. An employee should gather from this how all departments make up the sum of the agency and that no department works in isolation.
- A daily schedule that highlights what the employee's activities will consist of and who is responsible for overseeing them during the first one to two weeks (i.e. reviewing the department handbook from 9:00 a.m. to 12:00 p.m. with

Mary Smith, observing Jane Doe, a peer who is in the same position, from 1:00 p.m. to 4:00 p.m., etc.).

- Allow for 30 minutes to one hour the next day for employees to ask questions and process the events of the prior day. Be consistent in following through with this for your new employee, as they will have a great deal of information to process. While the employee is making the best first impression with you, you are also making a first impression upon them and attempting to build a positive relationship.

- Give the employee a good feel for the organization right from the beginning that the agency is organized and committed to their well-being. If possible, take the employee out for lunch on their first day. Spend as much time as possible with them so that they are comfortable and aware of what is expected of them. Poor orientation and training leads to employees who not only fail to provide high quality services to clients, but to decreased job satisfaction and longevity.

- After the orientation period, frequently check in with the employee to gather how they are adjusting to their new environment. The more time and interest you take in them, the more committed they will be to the department and agency. It is important to thoroughly communicate your interest in their development and how they are acclimating to their new environment (everyone adjusts to a new environment differently).

The initial investment of time and energy in effectively orienting staff will result in increased staff stability.

Have Quality and Consistent Supervision

Regularly scheduled supervision with staff is vital to having a quality program that provides exceptional client-centered services. By having regular and quality supervision with staff you promote a forum to review their work, provide feedback on their progress, growth, as well as establish and follow up on your expectations. Quality supervision also promotes open dialogue between you and your staff.

The basics of quality supervision include:

- Supervision should be held on a regular and consistent basis that aligns with the organization's approach. Some positions may require more frequent supervision meetings to review time-sensitive information (i.e. court hearings, case staffings, etc.). Minimally, supervision with employees should not occur less than one time per month.
- Supervision sessions should involve: review of cases or clients, actionable and observed feedback on performance, imparting information that is pertinent to the employee (i.e. agency updates, status of their training hours, etc.) and a discussion related to the overall development of the employee. Use the supervision time as an opportunity to point out areas in which staff are doing well and areas that they need to improve in. Do not be afraid to inform an employee that they are not meeting standards in a given area. Giving constructive criticism in an area that requires

improvement needs to be well thought out and carefully conveyed to staff. Be sure to provide plenty of support so that staff leaves a supervision session feeling motivated to make any needed changes. Ensure that you point out the positive aspects of an employee's performance as well.

- Ensure that you devote part of the supervision session to the professional development of the employee. Too often, supervision focuses on task completion (i.e. review of open cases, pending issues, etc.) and does not devote enough time to focusing on the employee's development and growth. Be sure to focus on at least one area (preferably chosen by the employee) that will encourage discussion and dialogue.

- Have a guideline that you want your staff to follow (i.e. pertinent case information, issues that need to be addressed, etc.) so that when they arrive at the supervision session they are providing the information you need. This will help to increase responsibility on the employee to provide necessary information and reduce time in which you probe for answers.

- Take time in between supervision sessions to be proactive and write down important points that you want to cover with your employees. This can prove especially helpful when there are topics that you want to cover with them, but may forget. Additionally, this will help you to be prepared and not "wing it" with them. Regardless of how busy you may be, this is imperative for quality supervision.

- Give yourself at least 15 to 30 minutes of preparation time before meeting with your staff. This will afford you the opportunity to formulate proper word choice when providing feedback, illustrate observable examples that relate to areas of need and improvement, and anticipate possible responses from all perspectives. Be mindful of how your feedback will be perceived by your staff.

- Periodically (i.e. quarterly) review your past supervision notes for each employee. This will enable you to monitor the growth of your supervision approach.

- Begin each supervision session by following up on tasks you asked them to complete during the last session. This demonstrates to your employees that you follow through on assignments and will hold them accountable for completing tasks within specific timeframes.

- Be sure that all feedback is well documented. Unfortunately, there are times when employees do not meet performance standards. As such, it is important that your supervision notes are as clear and detailed as possible when discussing employee performance. While it can be very uncomfortable providing negative feedback to an employee, it is part of being a supervisor. Ensure that requests and deadlines are very clear in your notes (i.e. John will complete the discharge summaries for Mary Smith and Susan Jones by Friday, May 10 at 2:00 p.m.). In a therapeutic setting this may ensure that treatment plan goals being met and reviewed in a timely manner. This will help to support you in the event that you need to pursue disciplinary action against an employee who is not meeting expectations. Additionally, be sure to note the outcome of requests and deadlines in the next supervision session (i.e. John completed the discharge summaries for Mary Smith and Susan Jones by the requested deadlines or John turned in the discharge summary for Mary Smith on time, but did not turn in Susan Jones' summary until Monday, May 13th. John was instructed on May 8th to turn in all discharge summaries by Friday, May 10th at 2:00 p.m.).

- For staff that are struggling to meet expectations, offer to have more frequent supervision with them. This will help provide additional support to staff, especially if they are having difficulty. Remember, it is your responsibility to develop your staff. However, this should be a short-term process for the ultimate solution of the employee meeting performance expectations.

- Provide field supervision on a regular basis (i.e. monthly), if possible. Observing your staff in action will provide first-hand information on performance and allow you the opportunity to provide real-time feedback to them.

- Periodically revisit the annual evaluation form and provide it to the employee, as well as review their progress in each category. Again, do not be afraid to provide real time feedback if an employee is struggling in an area. This is the perfect opportunity to provide guidance and support in how to improve performance.
- Have staff complete a self-assessment at the midpoint (i.e. six months) of each year. This will allow staff to reflect on their performance. If your staff's self-assessment contrasts with your observation of their performance, have them elaborate on these items during supervision sessions. Additionally, you can explore your observations and ratings with them. This helps to eliminate surprises at the time of the annual review. Ultimately, this provides the employee with ample time to improve any areas of need. If the performance evaluation is long and comprised of many questions, work with HR to develop a short version (i.e. five questions) where staff can focus on a few specific areas (i.e. customer service, problem solving, completion of tasks, etc.). If twice a year is too much, consider having employees complete a self-evaluation just before their annual evaluation is due.
- During supervision, write down your notes while the employee is present and be sure to sign it, and have them sign it as well. Once completed and signed, provide a copy to the employee for their records.
- Focus on listening more to your staff. Be cognizant to allow staff to fully explain their position/frustrations without having preconceived ideas or judgment. Moreover, resist the urge to offer a viewpoint/response before the employee is finished explaining the situation fully. Upon receiving an explanation from the employee, ask further questions to increase understanding of their perspective and/or response.
- Allow staff to vent without fear of retribution. There are times that staff may simply be frustrated and need to "let it out." When staff does vent provide them with a five-minute timeframe to let out their frustrations and do not interrupt.

Also, inform staff that it is acceptable for them to vent and it will not be held against them. Use these opportunities to challenge staff to devise creative ideas to decrease their stress levels (i.e. not taking things too personally, having improved boundaries, increasing their ability to turn down work, etc.).

Use of Performance Expectations: Job descriptions tend to be vague and do not provide clarity as to specific expectations of an employee in a given position. As such, take the time to develop performance expectations for your employee(s).

What to include in performance expectations:
- Expected production (i.e. how many cases to be opened per week, clients to be seen, etc.).
- Task related responsibilities and duties (what is expected to be completed for a new client intake, discharge, etc.)
- Timeliness in completing reports and paperwork (i.e. within five days of case closure).
- Behavioral expectations (i.e. displaying positive body language at all times, having a positive attitude, mentoring new team members, being on time for all meetings, how to professionally disagree with staff/management, sharing knowledge, etc.)

How to implement performance expectations:
- Performance expectations are documents that can be referred to in supervision sessions, especially if staff are not adhering to the standards of job performance.
- Upon completing performance expectations be sure to have the human resources department review them so that they are realistic and in compliance with agency standards.
- Deliver to employees and document in their supervision notes that they have been provided and reviewed with staff.
- Avoid having staff sign the document, as this will lead to less conflict if they do not agree with it.

Example Performance Expectation:

Shelter Coordinator Performance Expectations

Task Oriented Expectations

1. Be at work on time and work your assigned schedule. If you are going to be more than 10 minutes late, call your supervisor. If you are out sick, please call your supervisor before the beginning of your shift to notify them of your absence.
2. When out of the office ensure that the out-of-office reply is turned on for your email and your voicemail reflects you are out of the office, when you will return, and who to contact during your absence.
3. Request time off at least two weeks in advance.
4. Secure placement for children who are in shelters within 30 days.
5. Prioritize placement needs and efforts for children five and under. Provide the Assistant Director with latest placement updates/efforts each Monday by 10:00 a.m.
6. Ensure that all medical and mental health needs of children are being met. Assess each child in the shelter to see if they require further service intervention. If so, make appropriate referrals.
7. Work diligently to locate and secure placement for children. Approach all situations with a high sense of urgency and proactively work with Child Advocates and placement providers to secure placement for children in shelters.
8. Whenever you encounter barriers (i.e. Child Advocate/Child Advocate Supervisor not returning phone calls/emails within two business days) immediately escalate to your supervisor for assistance.
9. Ensure that all efforts are made to place children as close to their parents and siblings as possible and within their home school district.

10. Communicate (via phone or face-to-face) with Child Advocates at least weekly.
11. Document all placement efforts and contacts with Child Advocates/placement providers in FSFN within 48 hours of event.
12. Regularly update your personal spreadsheet on the M drive to thoroughly reflect prior placement efforts, barriers to finding placement, and current situation (i.e. visit scheduled).
13. Ensure appropriate services/referrals are in place when children transition from the shelter to their new placement.
14. Complete monthly reports, shelter visit notes, etc. in a timely and thorough manner.
15. Utilize critical thinking skills to proactively assess placement needs of children in shelters and to initiate contact with placement providers. If there is a barrier to finding placement (i.e. behavioral or developmental delay), use innovative thinking (i.e. thinking outside of the box) to help secure placement for the child(ren).
16. Schedule and attend placement interviews and visits as necessary.
17. Ensure that all emails are proofread and do not contain grammatical, spelling, and factual errors.
18. Complete Log of Logs entry for all placement movements. Ensure that the log is completed in its entirety and placed in the Log of Log book.
19. Complete bi-weekly visits and enter into FSFN for all children in shelters. Complete a Home Visit form for each child and ensure that it is entered into FSFN.
20. Check and respond to all email and phone calls daily.
21. Facilitate bi-weekly Shelter Staffings with foster home providers. Utilize the Provider Availability Report to assist with placements. Also, review 30-day notices with the providers.
22. Regularly review and utilize information on the shared drive (i.e. Provider Availability Report) to assist with placement efforts.

23. Keep your supervisor informed of any time-sensitive issues and escalate issues to your supervisor as appropriate.
24. Transport children to placement interviews as necessary.
25. Attend meetings on time and be knowledgeable of any issues surrounding the purpose of the meeting.
26. Ensure all tasks are completed with a high degree of quality and accuracy (i.e. Log of Logs entry, emails, case notes, etc.).
27. Meet all deadlines within expected time frames.
28. Inform your supervisor in a timely manner when any follow-up requests have been completed.
29. Take pride in completing all forms, emails, and tasks with a high degree of quality.
30. Work with a high sense of urgency to complete all required and follow-up tasks.
31. Personal phone calls are to be made while on break.
32. Limit computer usage to company business only.
33. It is your responsibility to read and understand what your job responsibilities are. If you are unsure of your job responsibilities/duties, you are expected to obtain clarification from your supervisor.
34. Complete all other duties as assigned.

Behavioral Expectations

1. Present with positive nonverbal body language at all times.
2. Actively engage, participate, and offer solutions during meetings and staffings.
3. Support management decisions. If you do not agree with a decision, speak to your supervisor individually about your concerns.
4. Offer solutions and ideas to help make the department more efficient.
5. Proactively assist and mentor new and existing team members.
6. Do not engage in gossip.

7.   Engage internal and external stakeholders in a highly professional, respectful, friendly, and a "make it happen" manner.

8.   Take pride in how you represent your department and agency.

9.   Handle issues with coworkers and/or supervisor privately. Be mindful of how your verbal and nonverbal behavior can be perceived by others.

Consistent and quality supervision will result in growth for your staff and optimized client care.

Performance Evaluations and Disciplinary Actions

Performance evaluations provide concrete feedback on employee performance. There are several implications involved in completing performance evaluations: whether or not the employee receives an increase in their salary, possibility for promotion, and support for the termination of an employee. Nevertheless, great care should be taken when completing an evaluation.

Providing disciplinary actions can be stressful and difficult to address. While one does not look forward to providing an employee with a disciplinary action, it is a necessary function of being a supervisor. Furthermore, when an employee does not meet expectations it affects other workers, the supervisor, clients, and the organization's credibility to the community. When an employee is not meeting performance expectations it strains an already burdened system by forcing others to compensate by increasing their workloads, which can negatively affect staff morale, satisfaction, and retention.

Ongoing evaluation and feedback can help minimize the need for disciplinary actions. Additionally, if a disciplinary action is required, the supervisor should communicate that it is an opportunity for growth and support the employee through the process, if they are open and receptive to it. Ultimately, if the employee does not see a disciplinary action as an opportunity for growth it may eventually lead to their termination.

Guidelines for effective completion of performance evaluations:

- Ensure that each section is fully and thoroughly completed. For example, be sure that each domain of the evaluation contains specific, objective, and observed behaviors.
  - If evaluating timeliness in completing tasks (meeting expectations): John completes reports by the due dates and typically submits them earlier than scheduled. John requires minimal prompting to complete tasks and submit work by the required deadlines. John exceeds the expectations for this area.
  - If the employee is not meeting expectations in a given area: John struggles with consistently submitting reports and paperwork by their assigned due dates. John typically gives numerous reasons that present as barriers to completing work on time. Furthermore, John struggles to take ownership of completing tasks timely. To meet expectations in this area John will submit all work by the assigned deadlines and/or proactively work with his supervisor to identify and eliminate barriers to completing work in a timely manner.
- Provide specific feedback on how employees can grow in each area. For example, if your organization's performance evaluation uses a five point scale and the employee receives a three in an area, provide concrete examples for how the employee can improve their performance.
  - If an employee struggles with knowledge of community resources, identify trainings that will enhance their knowledge.
- Include if the employee has received any accolades or disciplinary actions during the past year. These need to be addressed and clearly documented in the appropriate domain.
  - If an employee receives a disciplinary action during the year, provide documentation of the employee's progress since receiving said disciplinary action. From a human resource perspective it is imperative that performance evaluations accurately detail any

employee struggles, response to corrective action, etc.

- If the employee receives an accolade this needs to be clearly documented. It is important to reinforce employee strengths that led to them receiving the award/recognition.
- Evaluations should be fair, balanced, and objective. One should not allow personal differences/beliefs or personality conflicts with the employee to obscure objectivity.
- Provide an individualized plan for growth. It is important to include specifics on how the employee can grow during the next year.
    - For example, if an employee needs to improve their computer skills this should be noted. Assure that you follow up with training opportunities so to address any areas of need.
- When discussing the results of the performance evaluation with the employee it should come from a strength-based approach. Be sure to emphasize the strengths of the employee as well as how they contribute to the department and organization's performance and reputation. If you are reviewing an area of need it is vital to be precise and center on the facts surrounding their deficits. Moreover, move to how the employee can improve in the area and how you and the agency will support them in the process.
- Provide written definitions in advance to employees of what performance scores look like. This is an excellent way to help guide your staff to reach and exceed performance expectations and can be part of your vision for the department. For example, if an agency uses a one-five scale, a supervisor could provide their employees with the following information:
    - One (consistently not meeting expectations): Not following through on emails, follow-up requests, etc. Someone who receives a one in an area is experiencing a great deal of difficulty due to consistently not meeting performance expectations. This goes beyond making an occasional mistake.

- Two (not meeting expectations): An individual requires prompting and redirection to meet expected performance. They may lack initiative or demonstrate a consistent inability to follow through on assigned items without close supervision. This may also include an employee who submits work that consistently requires revision or who struggles with peer relationships/professional behavior.
- Three (meeting expectations): This is where an employee completes assigned tasks, submits work on time that requires minimal prompting, and requires minimal supervision. They can be counted on to complete tasks with little supervision needed. This may include completing files, home studies, treatment plans, on a satisfactory level. This individual completes what is expected of them.
- Four (exceeds expectations): This is where an individual consistently goes above and beyond what is expected of them. They present as an employee who actively seeks to improve their performance through feedback on improvement techniques and implementing suggestions that they receive. They also suggest how to modify or implement processes to help improve the efficiency and effectiveness of the unit and/or agency. When issues arise they are quick to assess the situation and offer up solutions when informing their supervisor. Employees who exceed expectations work with a high sense of urgency to complete tasks with a high degree of quality. Individuals who exceed expectations proactively look to initiate ways to assist coworkers while still completing their own duties. Individuals who fall into this category demonstrate consummate professionalism and are looked at, both internally and externally, as a team player.
- Five (exceptional performance): This is where an individual clearly stands out in a given area. This is where they consistently excel at a level that is well

above what is expected for the position. This looks like a four, but it is very consistent to the point that it is the general level of performance that this employee meets on a daily basis.

- Be a tough evaluator. Some supervisors do not provide accurate feedback to employees due to them avoiding conflict. More and more organizations are moving to raises that are performance based (i.e. based on performance evaluations) and if your organization has adopted this policy employees take their evaluations very seriously. Be clear with your department that meeting expectations is good, but if they want to earn scores that are above this range, they need to demonstrate behavior that goes above and beyond on a consistent basis.

The disciplinary action process:

- Disciplinary actions should be generated for situations including, but not limited to the following: insubordination, lack of professional conduct, not following agency policies and procedures, not meeting performance expectations, falsifying records, etc.
- As a supervisor one should be cognizant of situations that may require a disciplinary action. When in question consult with a peer, your supervisor and the human resources department. One should not avoid addressing critical issues that are listed above. There are times when a supervisor may be reluctant to pursue a disciplinary action due to their desire to avoid conflict/confrontation. It is important to note that ignoring situations that meet criteria for a disciplinary action will adversely affect the supervisor, other employees, the agency and the clients served.
- When writing a disciplinary action it is vital that one fully depicts the situation that occurred. The disciplinary action should be objective, factual, and concise (i.e. Mary has been late to work eight times over the last 30 days). Moreover, one needs to ensure that any emotional content has been eliminated. For example, if an employee demonstrates insubordinate behavior toward their supervisor, the anger

should not be evident when writing the disciplinary action. Give yourself time to refocus if needed.

- Once the disciplinary action has been completed by the supervisor, it should be reviewed by their supervisor and then sent to the human resources department for final review and approval. This will help to ensure that the disciplinary action meets all agency standards and allows for objective review.

- When delivering the disciplinary action with the employee be sure to have a peer or a representative from the human resources department present. One should never deliver a disciplinary action by themselves. The conversation should be initiated by the supervisor that is overseeing the employee and be brief, and then provided to the employee for review and signature. Remember, the less you say the better when delivering disciplinary actions to employees. Allow them to read what is written on the disciplinary action form, attain their signature, and provide them with a copy. If the employee refuses to sign the document have the witness document the employee's refusal to sign the document and end the meeting.

- If the employee disagrees with the disciplinary action, follow the agency policy and procedure regarding employee grievances. Be sure to communicate the agency policy regarding the appeal process for disciplinary actions. It is important for the employee to be heard and there are times when disciplinary actions are reversed after all the facts have been reviewed. However, one needs to work closely with their supervisor and the human resources department so that this does not occur, as it will negatively impact the supervisor's credibility with the employee and the rest of the department.

- A few days after the disciplinary action has been delivered to the employee, consider meeting with the employee to check with how they are processing the information. It is important to convey to the employee how they have been provided with the opportunity and the steps necessary to make improvements in their job performance. Moreover, it is also important to communicate your hope and desire that they will make progress and will provide whatever assistance to help them achieve this. Acknowledge that the work environment may be awkward, but addressing this will go a long way in helping the employee make needed changes and restore a sense of normalcy between the supervisor and the employee.

- There are times when a disciplinary action may be taken away. For example, if this is the first time that an employee has received a disciplinary action, consider working with your HR department to devise a strategy or plan that can lead to a win-win situation for the department and the employee.
  - For example, Mary was provided with a disciplinary action due to multiple reports from internal and external professionals of her rude and unprofessional behavior over a three-month period. She was provided with the opportunity to change her behavior and have the disciplinary action removed from her file. Mary was expected to demonstrate significant change as evidenced by pleasant and respectful interactions with individuals and no other reports/complaints of her behavior over a three-month period. Employees who have received a disciplinary action are typically highly motivated to ensure that this does not negatively impact their employment, so this is a strong motivator for change.
  - Be open to innovative ideas to help correct situations of performance issues, as this will only enhance employee commitment, retention, and performance.

Corrective Action Plans:

- Corrective Action Plans (CAP's) are typically implemented after an employee has received at least one disciplinary action and a consistent pattern of nonperformance exists.
- A CAP typically consists of:

- A thorough description of the issues and behaviors that are affecting the employee's performance.
- A statement that details what changes are needed.
- An action plan that describes specifically what the employee will do during the specified time period (usually 30-60 days). This may also include more frequent supervision. Be careful to not select a time period that is too short, as it may not provide adequate time for appropriate behavioral and/or performance change.
- The CAP should contain language that is approved by the human resources department that states that at the end of the plan the employee is expected to achieve skills required and if not, further disciplinary action up to and including termination will take place.

Terminations:

- There are times when despite all efforts an employee is not able to meet required expectations. It is vital for the supervisor to not see this as a failure on their part, but an unwillingness of the employee to grow. There may be some cases when immediate termination is mandatory due to the infraction (i.e. inappropriate contact with a client, fraud, theft, falsification of documents, etc.).
- As with any other disciplinary action one needs to have their supervisor and human resources department included in the determination to terminate an employee.
- In terms of meeting with a staff member who is going to be terminated, one should have another peer present or a member of the human resources department, depending on agency policy. The message to the employee should be short and direct informing them that due to their actions and/or inability to meet performance standards they will no longer be employed at the organization.
- After the termination has been delivered, a neutral party should escort the employee to their office to gather their belongings and then escort them out of the building. There

may be times, however, when an employee may need to be immediately escorted out and their personal belongs provided to them at a later date.

- After the employee has been terminated, one should inform the department that the employee is no longer with the agency because of nonperformance and/or violation of agency policy. One should not engage in a conversation with staff regarding the events surrounding the employee's termination. It is important to restore the work environment to a regular balance of performance as quickly as possible.
- Ensure that the rest of the agency is made aware that the selected employee is no longer employed with the organization. This can be through an email, memo, etc.

Effective performance plans provide necessary feedback for optimal employee growth.

Take Time to Develop Staff

Developing and implementing activities to increase the growth of staff is crucial to your unit and agency. By taking the time to develop your staff you, in turn, create an atmosphere for staff success. Additionally, time spent developing staff will lead to improved client care and the increased probability of them remaining with the organization. Taking the time to work with staff and facilitate improvement in their respective skill sets shows that you care and the agency is invested in their growth. Ultimately, you want to train your new and existing staff to be excellent leaders, which will increase their morale, desire to grow, and provide exceptional client care. Lastly, do not hesitate to create opportunities for employees who have verbalized a desire to grow and/or have applied for supervisory positions.

Ways to develop staff and show that you are committed to their development include:

- Provide literature, journal articles, and handouts related to specific skill sets necessary to improving performance (i.e. information on new treatments, trends, and philosophies). Pay attention to what staff is requesting regarding their training needs.
- Identify and offer opportunities for staff to attend specific trainings that will enhance their abilities to meet the needs of clients. Afterwards, provide a forum for staff to share any knowledge gained from trainings with colleagues, as this will help to increase the overall skill sets for the entire department and/or agency.

- If you identify employees who are ready or eager for promotion, provide opportunities for them to enhance their skill sets. This can be accomplished by having them take the lead on training opportunities (i.e. having them read an article and then providing a brief training on it to the rest of the department, take the lead with specific department tasks, etc.). Providing situations for growth helps to demonstrate initiative and willingness to grow. This also helps to create an optimal environment for employee satisfaction and commitment.

- Ask staff to complete a self-assessment to evaluate their performance approximately every three to six months. Review the self-assessment in a timely manner and provide appropriate feedback regarding their performance. Provide staff with evidence to justify areas for improvement (i.e. inform staff of behaviors that you have observed, not heard, so the feedback is valid). Also, provide concrete examples to support your views. This will help the employee see real examples, not general statements (i.e. "Your paperwork needs to improve." vs. "Your monthly reports have been late three out of the past four months.").

- Devise a development plan with employee input so as not to see this as a punitive measure or a process that will reflect negatively on their performance. This is a tool to genuinely help them grow based on the results of their self-assessment.

- Ideally, every employee should have a development plan at all times that is continually reviewed for adjustments to maximize their growth. The ongoing development plan can center on one to two areas and/or competencies, and can be regularly added or subtracted based on employee need and achievement. Be consistent in adding this to the supervision process so that it is reviewed regularly. Examples include being more approachable, problem-solving skills, computer skills, etc.

- Setting high expectations for your staff as well as encouraging them to set high expectations for themselves will also challenge them to reach new levels of performance and commitment.

- Champion outstanding work that goes beyond simply meeting standards, and challenge staff to exceed goals for themselves and for the department. Make it a habit to point out the excellent work that your staff performs, whether individually, through department/agency emails, or during meetings. This will reinforce how valuable staff is and how their efforts are appreciated. Be cognizant of how to recognize employees based on their comfort levels with receiving praise. For example, some employees may get embarrassed by receiving public acknowledgement versus private recognition.
- Encourage staff to demonstrate everyday leadership through taking initiative to meet client needs, solve issues in the department, and offer solutions to challenges and barriers. Regardless of one's position, this skill can be consistently exhibited starting with clerical staff and up through the rest of the department. Leadership is defined by one's behavior and not limited to one's position and/or title.
- Use a solution focused approach. A solution focused approach emphasizes the strengths that your employees demonstrate. Also, use solution focused language with staff such as, "If things were working well, what would they look like?" This is a useful question to challenge staff on how to approach situations.
- Look at every opportunity to engage staff as a teachable moment, in how can they learn something and transfer it to future situations. Capitalize on the strengths of staff and use this to build on. Additionally, identify three to five skills or competencies they perform well in so that they are aware of their strengths.
    - For example, if an employee struggles with utilizing critical thinking skills to achieve a better outcome, review the entire situation with the employee. One can use a decision tree process with the employee to review at junctures of the situation how different decisions could have been made to achieve a better outcome.

- Coach staff and guide them to assess a concern or need and then formulate potential solutions. This will encourage employees to become independent and proactive in their abilities to solve situations. This also allows them to feel successful in empowering clients as well as fostering a sense of competency for the employee. Acknowledge this achievement when they demonstrate the ability to proactively problem solve issues.
- Use the "sandwich technique" when addressing situations for improvement with your staff. The sandwich technique is composed of: initially recognizing a positive attribute or a successful situation of the employee and praising them, addressing a concern that needs to be addressed, and finishing by reinforcing a positive attribute or successful situation of the employee.
- Be excited. Leaders that demonstrate passion for what they do stand a good chance to have this spread throughout the department and/or agency.
- Remember, though, in order to develop your staff you must be committed to developing yourself. Openly discuss trainings that you have attended or books that you have read to show your staff you practice what you preach. As a leader, it is your role to model the proper approach.

**Developing staff will create an atmosphere
of success and commitment
to your vision.**

Maximizing Department Performance

Attaining a consistently high level of performance from your department is among the many challenges that leaders in the human services face. There are many obstacles and challenges that will interfere with peak staff performance, but your role is to find ways to resolve them. Effective human service organizations are comprised of leaders who find creative ways to motivate, energize, and support their employees.

How to maximize department performance:
- Clarify tasks and assignments as well as clearly communicate your expectations. Write down what staff is expected to accomplish so that there is no misunderstanding. For example, sending out emails after meetings is an excellent way to clarify who is responsible for specific tasks.
- Identify barriers, challenges, and/or obstacles for staff and find ways to remove them or provide alternatives. Effective human service leaders can identify any roadblocks to service delivery and find ways for staff to accomplish tasks more efficiently (i.e. streamlining the paperwork needed to complete an intake).
- Be outcome oriented. Many funders focus only on outputs, so it is imperative that you have an outcome oriented approach where staff can quantify their work. For example, holding staff accountable to open up at least four new cases per month.

- Develop monthly goals for the department. This will help to involve each member of your unit and provide them with a unified goal (i.e. license four new foster homes per month, maintain a specific amount of clients per month for each employee, discharge a specific amount of clients from probation, etc.). Shared goals help individuals within the department to take ownership and responsibility for the outcome.
- Frequently praise employees. Make it a habit to catch staff performing well. This will help to reinforce positive and productive behavior.
- Be prepared for change. Change within the human services field is inevitable. Unfortunately, staff often have difficulty when change occurs and it is your role to effectively and positively message this to staff so that client care, morale and productivity does not suffer.
- Ask probing questions. Effective leaders ask the right questions that help staff arrive at thoughtful conclusions. While it may be tempting to provide input or the solution when presented with a situation, use questions to help staff develop their own thought processes.
    - For example, if an employee completes a home visit for a potential relative placement, ask questions to lead the employee to independently assess and arrive at the conclusion if the placement is appropriate or not.
- Have quarterly meetings with staff to discuss department morale, barriers/challenges that employees are experiencing, as well as solutions to issues. After setting the ground rules for the meeting (i.e. how to appropriately verbalize frustration), allow staff to freely discuss their issues. Ensure that employees understand that there will be no retribution on your part for any feedback provided. Additionally, be sure to follow through on any feedback or ideas provided as appropriate. This is different from a monthly staff meeting, as it focuses solely on the employees.

Delegate

- Be mindful that you cannot do everything yourself, even if you can do it more efficiently than your staff. A successful human services leader can delegate, guide, and support their staff. Provide small opportunities at first for your staff to complete tasks and after observing positive staff performance relinquish more duties for staff to complete. Communicate your expectations for the task in writing, if possible, and then allow them to complete it within a specific time frame. It is important that you do not micromanage your staff and check in informally (i.e. ask them, "How are things going? Is there anything that I can assist with?"). Only review the work when it is completed, then provide feedback based on your observations and the quality of what they have done.
- Successful delegation enables your staff to grow and for you to focus on more innovative ways to improve client care.
- Many direct line workers are promoted due to their strong work ethic, commitment to high quality client care, and track record for achieving positive outcomes. However, the circumstances change once you become a supervisor. You can no longer single-handily complete tasks, but have to motivate and train your staff to complete them with a high degree of quality.

Many human service leaders run into problems because they feel they have to do too much of the work on their own due to the following:

- Inability to adequately train staff
- Lack of time to train staff
- Fear of having to confront staff who are not meeting expectations
- Fear that staff will not complete tasks the way they would

If you have staff that are not performing and you have to do their work for them, then this needs to be addressed right away. Work with your supervisor, peers, or the human resources department for support and guidance on how to address poor performing staff.

The consequences of ineffective delegation include:

- Increased job difficulty and feelings of being overwhelmed due to taking on extra responsibilities
- Resentment toward underperforming staff and the agency as a whole
- Continued poor performance from staff
- Decreased credibility with department staff and upper management
- Supervisor burnout and turnover

Effective human service leaders find innovative ways to motivate their staff and to maximize department performance.

Plan, Suggest, and Facilitate Effective Trainings

In many human service organizations employees often complain about the lack of trainings offered and lack of diversity in trainings that are provided. This rings especially true if you are a service provider and need to stay on top of cutting-edge practices in relation to working with clients. Many agencies commonly provide the same mandatory trainings to their staff each year and then wonder why staff does not grow and learn different tools to engage clients. A common barrier to facilitating effective trainings is the budgetary constraints that are associated with staff development. This is a sad fact knowing that little money and time is often spent on developing caring, competent staff and providing them with the tools to be successful at their jobs.

Having fun, relevant, and interactive trainings are essential to developing staff. Employees need to work in an environment that is truly committed to their growth. As such, the department and agency are responsible for ensuring that employees have the trainings they need to be as successful as possible. While budgetary constraints are a common issue experienced by all organizations, it is the responsibility of the agency to either find inexpensive or free trainers, or train the management team so that they can facilitate quality trainings.

Important points to consider regarding trainings:

- Quality trainings are a foundation to a successful organization. Having meaningful and thought provoking trainings convey to employees that the agency is committed to them and their growth. This goes a long way to improving morale and a commitment to exceptional client care.
- Many trainings are required annually, however a varied approach and willingness of staff to learn or perfect a basic skill set are of utmost importance. Be especially mindful of this so that you can instill in your staff the importance of trainings and how they can help improve the delivery of services to clients.
- There should be a sentiment in the department that staff looks forward to upcoming trainings to increase their knowledge and skill set. Interactive, fun, and dynamic trainings will help to accomplish this goal.
- Seek to reinforce important points learned from various trainings throughout the year so that key information from a particular training is not forgotten. This can be accomplished through reinforcing several different principles per month in a memo, newsletter, email, or on a poster.
    - For example, if staff attend NAPPI training (Non Abusive Psychological and Physical Intervention) annually, there should be ongoing reminders regarding the skills and concepts gained.
- For agencies that have a limited training budget, quality trainings rest on the management team. See if the agency will send members of the management team to specific trainings so they can become a trainer to agency staff.
- It is important to survey staff as to their training needs and interests. Using a simple questionnaire or sending an email to all staff on a quarterly basis can help accomplish this. This gives recognition to staff that the management team is listening and interested in what staff needs to help them grow and serve clients more effectively.
- Collaborate with local government agencies or other providers to conduct trainings at your agency. Sometimes organizations can exchange trainings with each other. This

will help to improve coordination and collaboration between agencies within the community.

- Be mindful that many government agencies conduct trainings for free or at very low cost. Check the agency training calendars regularly for trainings that you feel would be helpful to you or your staff.
- Have your agency subscribe to key journals in the field (i.e. *Child Welfare*, *Social Work*, etc.). This will allow the agency to stay abreast of new and innovative trends within the field. Any information read in these journals should be disseminated to staff.
    - For example, upon reading a research article from a journal have staff get together during a lunch hour and discuss the journal article and how it can be applied toward a current client.
- Purchase a book or have each member of the management team obtain one, or see if a select employee will read a book or an article on a different topic, and then provide training to staff. This is a good opportunity to further your knowledge while training staff on cutting-edge skills and techniques. If you select this option, converting your notes into a PowerPoint presentation may prove to be helpful.
- If you conduct trainings, be sure to be interactive, energetic, and motivated. Individuals who merely read off the material do not get much participation and the message that is conveyed is that the training is unimportant. Engage the group with icebreakers, schedule group activities, and ask the group questions throughout the training so that participation is optimal. Ultimately, participants should be able to walk away from the training with the ability to immediately utilize the knowledge gained.
- For example, if providing training it is imperative to engage the group in a manner that will lead to thoughtful discussion and dialogue. This can be accomplished through: role-plays, small group discussion, evaluation of a vignette, providing opportunities for participants to demonstrate the knowledge that they have learned from the training, and

intentionally providing an incorrect solution to a situation to help generate discussion.

Effective training promotes, maintains, and retains high quality staff.

Develop a Vision for your Program

A vision is a concept that may never be achieved, but a goal that you always strive for. Think of a vision as the highest level of organizational functioning that can be attained. Furthermore, a vision provides unified goals for you and your department. When you look to put a vision together for your program, operate from the standpoint of what the program would look like if it was functioning at an optimal level, the best that it could possibly be. What would an optimally run department look like if you walked into the office? How would the office look? How would your staff be behaving? How would staff be interacting with each other? How would staff be interacting with clients? How would staff be interacting with external stakeholders? All of these are concepts that you want to have answered in your vision so it spells out exactly what everyone should be striving for.

Undoubtedly, your organization will have a mission and vision. However, that does not mean that you cannot form a vision for your specific department that compliments the vision of your agency. In fact, putting a vision together will only strengthen your department and give all staff a unified purpose. Additionally, one can always revert back to the vision if it appears, for example, that the department's morale is low or staff is struggling with an event that has occurred in the agency.

Potential concepts that a program vision can cover include:

- Staff behavior (very helpful, outgoing, friendly, readily willing to go above and beyond for clients and coworkers, taking pride in the work they do, etc.).
- Do not be afraid to generate lofty goals for your vision. It is meant to be a tool that you and your staff can refer back to if you feel the program is losing its focus.
- Utilize your vision as a motivational tool to create and enhance staff performance and buy-in. This will make your interactions with staff more program and client focused.
    - For example, communicate to staff how a component of the department's vision is related to day-to-day activities (i.e. how client surveys can support one's vision that clients feel respected).
- Ideally, you do not want to have more than a page of information so that it can be easily displayed and referenced.
    - For example, the finished vision should be displayed throughout the department (i.e. on bulletin boards, posters, etc.).
- A vision is ever-evolving and needs to be flexible for changing conditions.
- After completing the first draft of your vision, share it with your staff and see if they have any ideas to add. This will increase their buy-in as well as show staff that you are an inclusive leader.

Sample Vision

Intake Department Vision

- Demonstrate exceptional customer service, responsiveness, attitude, body language, and professionalism to internal and external stakeholders at all times.
- Consistently demonstrate a "make it happen" and solution-oriented approach to solving client and organizational issues.
- Proactively anticipate and respond to any problems that may arise.
- When issues arise that you are involved in, offer solutions to solve the problem.
- Take initiative to offer solutions to enhance client care and department/agency performance (continuous quality improvement).
- Possess a strong desire to be part of the department/agency team.
- Be a team player and seek to assist colleagues whenever possible.
- Initiate exceptional collaboration with all internal staff as well as external stakeholders. Internal and external stakeholders should seek us out due to our knowledge and ability to effectively navigate situations.
- Think "outside of the box" to resolve client and organizational issues.
- Be experts in community resources and have all contact information at your fingertips to assist colleagues or providers.
- Make optimal placement decisions for youth that will enable them to be with their siblings, close to family, and remain in their school districts. Use all available information to assist (i.e. Bed Availability Report, etc.).
- Employees seek ways to enhance their personal and professional growth by attending internal/external trainings and/or furthering their education.

- All written work (reports, spreadsheets, emails, etc.) is of exceptional quality. They are free of spelling/grammatical errors and contain all vital information that individuals are able to read without the need to ask further questions.
- Ensure that department personnel are communicating at a high level (i.e. IPA's exchanging information verbally and in writing during shift change, etc.).
- Freely share information with colleagues and providers. If you attend trainings, present the information learned to your coworkers.
- Take pride in the quality of your work. Be proud of your professional reputation and the reputation of the department/agency in the community.

Being vision oriented provides purpose and commitment.

Seek Support and Guidance from Peers

Having the support of peers is one of the best ways to learn and grow as a leader. When you are able to have a close relationship with at least one peer, it allows for the opportunity to share ideas and provide feedback to one another. By having a peer to consult with, it will decrease feelings of isolation due to being the lone decision maker for staff issues. This will also minimize the need to go to your direct supervisor as frequently and to take more initiative to solve matters. One should always keep their supervisor informed of important events occurring within your department; however, there is nothing wrong with consulting with a peer ahead of time so that they can get guidance from them on how to proceed. This is especially true if the peer has been with the agency longer and knows specific policies and procedures, or how similar events have been addressed in the past. Furthermore, it allows you to receive feedback on situations that you may regret by handling on your own (i.e. sending out an inappropriate email to an individual that you are frustrated with).

Important aspects in developing positive peer relationships:
- Try to seek out at least one peer with whom you can meet formally or informally and be committed to helping each other grow. Ideally, it is the type of relationship in which you can both challenge each other and address areas for improvement. A quality peer relationship will allow you to

discuss the frustrations that you may be experiencing. Be mindful to limit your focus on frustrations and quickly look for solutions to the issue(s) so that it does not become a negative forum.

- Form a supervisory support group. This is a forum that can meet monthly for a couple of hours and be led by a more senior peer. A supervisory support group is designed to cover topics each individual and department is dealing with (i.e. an underperforming employee, difficulty increasing referrals, addressing low morale, reinforcing the department's vision, etc.) and provide each other with useful feedback on how to handle situations. Support groups present as a good opportunity for individuals who have a mixture of experience to collaborate. Be mindful that the group adheres to strict confidentiality so that information shared about a specific employee does not get back to them.

Seek out a Mentor

- Very few individuals are able to advance without the help of a mentor. Take time to seek out veteran peers or supervisors and request time to meet with them periodically. This will provide an opportunity to vicariously learn from them. Ideally, one can also ask to engage in a formal mentoring relationship with an individual. Mentoring relationships shows your willingness to learn, as well as provides key insight from others who possess a great deal of experience.
- Mentors can also be sought externally as well; this can come in the form of former supervisors, colleagues, etc. Take the initiative to seek out individuals that you respect in the community and see if you can meet up for lunch periodically to "pick their brain."
- Spend time with employees who are leaving the agency to gain insight and understanding from their perspective. This may hold especially true for individuals who have been with the agency for a long period of time and are leaving on a positive note. Use your judgment regarding

spending time with individuals that are disgruntled and have a negative perception of the agency.

Mentoring relationships provide key insight and support to assist with growth and development.

Work Closely with Functional Teams

Client care is only one function of a successful human services organization. Other functions include: human resources, fundraising/marketing, information technology, staff development, finance, and quality management. These functional teams are essential to the vitality of a successful agency. While each function operates independently, the success of the organization depends also on how well they work together.

Human Resources (HR)

Depending on how the agency operates, you will work very closely with the HR team.

Situations in which you will need the help of HR vary, but typically include:

- Having to provide a disciplinary action to an employee.
- Hiring or terminating an employee.
- Developing a Corrective Action Plan for an employee.
- Preparing an annual review or probationary evaluation for an employee.
- Dealing with miscellaneous issues such as workman's compensation, Family Medical Leave Act, etc.

Other aspects of how working closely with the HR department can be beneficial include:

- Whenever possible, try to process all pertinent information with the HR department before delivering it to your staff. Moreover, it is typically in your best interest to keep HR informed of all employee related matters ahead of time. By not keeping HR informed of pertinent employee related events in your department, you run the risk of making decisions that may have to be overturned later on and cause you to lose credibility (i.e. providing an evaluation to an employee who is not meeting standards, but your supervision notes do not adequately document their deficiencies. If you deliver the evaluation to them without the proper documentation to support your evaluation, the employee may file a grievance and your initial decision may be overturned or open the agency to potential litigation).

- Seek feedback from the HR department, as well as your supervisor, especially when dealing with employees who are not meeting performance standards. HR personnel have expertise in handling employee issues. They tend to have a more global and unbiased view of issues as compared to those who have more of a relationship with a specific employee.

Fundraising/Marketing

The fundraising/marketing team is an integral member of your agency, as many programs may run a deficit and require financial assistance to achieve financial vitality. It is important to work closely with the fundraising/marketing team, as they are the ones who interact with the general public and bring in vital revenue. This department can seek grants for your specific program or client needs.

A few ways to work closely with the Fundraising/Marketing team include:

- Offer to attend events to support the department. While attending events may take you or your staff away from serving clients or outside of normal work hours, always remember that they are the ones who bring in needed revenue for the agency.

- Be mindful that the fundraising/marketing department's perspective may differ from that of a department that provides direct service and must be respected (i.e. their priorities are different than yours). The more knowledge that they have about your department, the better they can present your story to the community.
- Provide requested statistical data to support the need for continued funding for grants and financial support.
- Their relationship with the community and access to volunteers can offer specific assistance, such as attaining food, toys, clothing, furniture, etc., for your clients.

Quality Management (QM)

If your agency has a quality management department, then you are fortunate. If not, this will be part of your department's responsibility. The QM department's role is to ensure that all quality standards are being followed. If your organization is accredited by The Council on Accreditation (COA), the QM department will serve a vital role in ensuring the agency meets these standards on an ongoing basis.

The QM department can assist with the following:

- Auditing client files.
- Preparing for external audits.
- Making quality phone calls to clients to receive feedback on employee performance and satisfaction with services.
- Developing systems to increase efficiency.
- Developing internal surveys to assess staff satisfaction. Surveys can be developed internally or through services such as www.surveymonkey.com. It is important to inform staff that surveys completed are anonymous. This will help staff to provide honest feedback without fear of retribution. The QM department should also develop surveys to provide to external stakeholders (i.e. other agencies, funders, clients,

etc.) to obtain feedback on agency performance and collaboration. Survey results need to be carefully reviewed and changes should be implemented from the feedback for this to be a successful tool in the future. At a minimum, surveys should be used every six-twelve months and the results shared with staff.

- Do not hesitate to request a periodic file review, quality calls to clients, or an objective look at your tracking systems to help increase efficiency in your department. Remember, they are on your team to assist and support programs in running as smoothly and efficiently as possible.

Information Technology (IT)

The IT department works behind the scenes, but is equally important. They make sure the servers are working, address any email issues, troubleshoot issues with program applications, etc. They are tasked with supporting the entire agency, not just individual departments or staff.

The IT department can assist with the following:

- Setting up a work station for a new or existing employee (i.e. email, phone, internet, etc.). Be sure to provide as much notice as possible when making IT requests so all requests can be completed within a timely manner.
- Developing applications or programs to increase department efficiency (i.e. developing a program to track referrals).
- If you have employees who you suspect are surfing the web too much, do not hesitate to ask the IT department to examine their internet activities (it is recommended that agencies have a computer usage agreement to address agency computer usage expectations). Always be sure to request that they review the whole department for internet use so you are equitable in your approach.

Finance Department

The finance department is responsible for the development of budgets, projections, issuing checks, petty cash, payroll, and mileage/various expenses.

The Finance Department Can Assist With the Following:

- Keeping you abreast of your year-to-date budget figures to address adjustment of revenue and expenses.
- Processing reimbursement claims (i.e. Medicaid-eligible services).
- Processing of timely corrections to payroll issues.
- Payment of trainings, seminars, and mileage reimbursement.

A well-rounded manager must understand the importance of functional teams and how they support overall department and agency functioning.

Facilitate Efficient and Productive Meetings

A human services leader will be involved in many meetings. The types of meetings that you will attend may include: client related, staff related, department, and/or organizational in nature. As such, it is essential that you, as a supervisor, facilitate quality meetings. As a supervisor, staff and peers will look to you to be organized, efficient, and results oriented when running meetings, so it is vital that you commit to making this one of your strengths.

Aspects of a quality meeting include:

- Have an agenda that will enhance discussion and encourage input from all participants attending the meeting. The agenda should be forwarded to meeting participants ahead of time to encourage discussion and knowledge of the issues.
- Have a purpose for why the meeting is being held. This should be stated at the onset of the meeting to help clarify for all individuals a sense of what the focus of the group will be as well expected outcomes.
- Possess history and updated knowledge of the issues (do your homework ahead of time and do not just show up and "wing it"). Obtain current knowledge and status of the situation (i.e. where is the child currently placed, when is the client scheduled to be released, when is the client funded through, etc.).

- Obtain and validate the concerns and viewpoints of all parties. Ensure that all meeting participants have an opportunity to provide their input.
- Keep the group on task by redirection back to the original purpose of the meeting. This will be an ongoing challenge to keep meeting participants on task throughout your time together.
- Maintain an ability to reach a consensus even if some members do not agree. Depending on the type of meeting being held and severity of the issues being discussed, one needs to be cognizant of the opposing views. These views will subsequently be evaluated to help the group reach consensus to resolve any issues. Some issues may not be able to be resolved during the course of the meeting and this does not mean that the meeting was not successful.
- Facilitation skills are a must. Become adept at facilitating meetings to help them remain on task and meet pre-arranged objectives. Do not be afraid to step in and mediate if necessary.
- Separate meetings may need to be held to address issues that may not be able to be resolved in one meeting. This is a common strategy when individuals may posture themselves to be initially unreceptive to a proposed resolution. However, having an additional meeting may provide time to hold a forum for reflection, research information and data for validity, and an evaluation of the proposed resolution and/or amendment to the initial resolution.
- Summarizing at the end of the meeting what was discussed and who is accountable for what tasks, providing written documentation of information, and concerns to all parties. Additionally, it is important to point out who will be following up on designated activities in a specific timeframe at the end of the meeting or shortly thereafter in written or email (i.e. scanning and forwarding the notes to all meeting participants).
- As the leader, identify individuals that have been assigned to follow up on agreed agenda items as well as any follow up tasks that have been discussed. Ensure that these items

are completed in a timely manner. This is a key component that is sometimes lacking and will help you to stand out if you make it an area of strength.

Guidelines for a quality staff meeting:

- Provide agenda to staff before the meeting. This will enable them to review/be prepared for the meeting.
- When preparing the agenda be cognizant to allow for open discussion. Assure there is ample time allotted for open discussion.
- The agenda should include, but is not limited to:
  - Review of minutes from the last meeting and ensuring accuracy
  - Review of select policies and procedures
    - Select a few agency policies and procedures to review each meeting to increase staff knowledge.
  - Review of department trends and data
    - For example, review how cases were received for the prior month, progress with department/agency outcome measures, etc. Sharing any data with staff can assist with having shared goals to improve outcome measures.
  - Discussion of important department issues and concerns
    - For example, if an issue is identified that is negatively impacting department performance be mindful to bring it up in a manner so that staff understands how the issue is affecting the department (i.e. intake files not being completed in a timely manner and how this negatively effects the overall case assignment process). After identifying the issue, have the group problem solve how the issue can be corrected.
    - When identifying issues make sure that all employees are adhering to any department/agency changes and when the updated process will take effect.

- Employee recognition (be sure to point out any employee successes)
  - Make an effort to acknowledge instances of employees going above and beyond as well as when the department exceeds expectations.
  - Name an employee of the month (this is recommended to help increase staff morale). Consider using an item or trophy that can be passed on to the employee each month.
  - Acknowledge employee birthdays and anniversaries.
  - Encourage employees to give positive feedback to one another and give kudos for jobs well done.
- Training opportunities and sharing information that is pertinent to job area
  - For example, if an employee attends training or receives training material, provide an opportunity for them to present this to the rest of the team.
- Discussion of agency updates
- Open forum
- Be mindful how employees process information and to customize your message accordingly (i.e. some employees are visual learners, others auditory, etc.).
- Focus on ending each meeting on a positive note (i.e. thanking staff for their time, sharing positive feedback from a provider/client, etc.).

**Meetings with a purpose
and a goal produce
effective results.**

Establish Quality Relationships with Internal and External Stakeholders

Supervisors will have contact with many different individuals and agencies. An external stakeholder may be in the form of a funder or agencies that work with your clients in a different capacity. Having quality relationships with external stakeholders and funders is essential because it helps to enhance client care and build your personal credibility, as well as the credibility and reputation of the agency.

From an internal perspective, it is important that you have a good relationship with your staff as well as all employees within your agency. Your approach to working with others will be vital to your success at your present position and will affect your ability for promotion, if that is your goal. As such, you want to be a pro-teamwork individual and encourage your staff to have this perspective. While many verbalize their understanding of teamwork and can state what positive teamwork looks like, many cannot put this into action. Be mindful the proof of you being a pro-teamwork individual will be evaluated by your actions. Teamwork is not confined to one specific department, but should be visible between all departments and individuals throughout the agency (i.e. line staff to supervisors to directors).

Ways in which you can establish or improve relationships with external stakeholders include:

- Make it a point to attend and actively participate in monthly or quarterly provider meetings. This will give you an opportunity to have a thorough knowledge of who key individuals are in the community and what their roles are. Additionally, it will allow you to interact with other professionals and develop relationships that may help increase referrals, find out information about a potential hire, or lead to other opportunities.
- Volunteer to participate in workgroups, both with mutual providers and within the community.
- Reach out to community providers to periodically schedule lunch meetings. This will enhance networking opportunities. Having a personal relationship with external stakeholders also increases collaboration. When a critical situation occurs, this collaboration and relationship can assist with resolving issues (i.e. needing assistance with emergency placements). Be mindful to ensure that professional boundaries are adhered to at all times.
- Seek out other providers in the community who provide the same or similar services as your agency and maintain periodic contact to see how both agencies can mutually benefit each other. This may come in the form of referrals (they may get full and rather than have a waitlist, they can send the referrals to your agency or vice versa), exchanging information or training resources. Collaboration is a key element that is sometimes missing in the field. Excelling in this area will set you apart from others and allow for relationship building.
- If you are working with a funder, be mindful that the best way to have a great relationship with them is to be their "go to" person. A "go to" person is someone that is responsive to phone calls, inquiries, processing documents with a high sense of quality and urgency, etc. By being able to consistently have positive client outcomes, quality client files, and communicating effectively with funders you put yourself

and your agency in a better position to maintain contracts as well as expand if the funds are available.

- For example, a provider that can take difficult to work with clients, therapy providers that are willing to take clients above their available case load, agencies that are willing to see clients beyond normal business hours, foster care agencies that can place sibling groups, teenagers, etc.

- Take the initiative to personally visit contacts at funding agencies or other community providers. Also, do not hesitate to invite funders or community providers to your agency. Having a face-to-face meeting with individuals from funders or other agencies strengthens your relationship with them and helps with problem solving opportunities.
- Always return phone calls and emails promptly. Try to use the phone more than email so that you can establish a close relationship with your respective contact(s).
- If you have an issue with your funder point of contact, be as diplomatic and respectful as possible, and remember how essential it is to have a positive relationship with your funder. It is acceptable to have a difference of opinion with your contact, but do so in an "agree to disagree" manner.
- Work closely with your staff to ensure that they are always mindful to be pleasant, prompt and professional with funders and other community stakeholders.
- Be diplomatic during community meetings. Individuals that can add thoughtful insight, perspective, and solutions during meetings can quickly gain credibility in the community.

How to become more involved with internal team members:

- Volunteer to participate in any groups or committees that your agency has (i.e. safety, employee appreciation, etc.).
- Reach out to internal team members to go to lunch periodically. This will support informal collaboration, which will be beneficial to agency and department productivity as well

as client care. Remember to adhere to professional boundaries when outside of the work environment.

- Make a suggestion to form a work group to address specific issues within the agency (i.e. to develop a staff supervision form, improve an existing form, evaluate systems, etc.).

- You will attend many meetings about client progress or ones focused on organizational goals and objectives. Either way, you want to take advantage of these settings to work collaboratively with others. Do not be inactive during these meetings. If you are not knowledgeable about specific topics that are covered, do your homework ahead of time so you are up to speed when the meeting is held.

- Do not be afraid to share your ideas during meetings. The only way to improve service delivery is to take risks and venture outside the box of conventional wisdom. This will help to promote discussion and challenge the thoughts and ideas of others; challenge the status quo. Always be sure to be respectful of the ideas of others and the existing systems that are in place.

- If you work at a large agency that spans different locations, try to form relationships with your counterparts. Additionally, have a conference call with them at least every couple of months to see how they are progressing on similar projects or programs. This can allow for the sharing of forms, processes, etc. There is no use recreating a process if someone else on your team is already using a form or approach that is very successful.

- If you work at a statewide agency that has the same program(s) in multiple locations, try to organize a monthly or quarterly conference call where information, forms, concerns, and ideas can be shared. This is an excellent opportunity to collaborate with individuals who are managing the same or similar programs.

Maintaining effective relationships with internal and external stakeholders will benefit the client and your agency.

Be Data Driven

Data collection and analysis is oftentimes an area of opportunity that the human services field struggles with. Focusing on objective data enables agencies to develop concrete guidelines and benchmarks for measuring success. Typically, many supervisors do not pay close attention to establishing or measuring outcomes, and this places the agency at a disadvantage for progressing and evolving from the standpoint of improving clients and gaining/maintaining credibility.

Focusing on data does not mean that client care suffers. The fact is the human services field has evolved into much more than a focus on client care. Agencies that can accurately collect and interpret data stand a better chance to receive funding due to the shift toward detailed evidenced-based outcome measures.

Useful tools to become more data oriented:
- Review any data that is collected to ascertain if the approach of the department or agency needs to be reassessed. Involve staff in these discussions so that they have the opportunity to provide their input.
- Use spreadsheets and/or data programs to track data and trends. Some agencies have each department complete a monthly standardized spreadsheet detailing a variety of client information such as:
  - referrals received
  - admissions
  - discharges
  - clients seen

- revenue generated
- client demographics
- client satisfaction surveys
- client goals achieved
- client success after discharge

- Develop PowerPoint/Excel charts to track information. This will allow you to have a quick reference point to look at trends from month to month and provides a reference point when evaluating data (i.e. being able to see a downward trend in referrals or clients served). This is another tool that is useful to provide to your supervisor, board of directors, and funders to keep them informed of trends and developments in your department.
- Track outcome measures to demonstrate client successes. By monitoring client progress after they are discharged from the program (i.e. at three months, six months, etc.) you can have support in reporting how successful your program is. If outcome measures show that clients are struggling after discharge, this supports the need for lengthening the program or funding other services to support clients post-discharge.
- Work to develop a comprehensive monthly department or agency report that can capture important information and trends (revenue, clients served, client demographics, etc.).

Collect as much data as possible so that a clear and concise picture can be drawn. This will enable the department and the agency to quickly identify trends and adjust to them.

Data drives accountability and credibility, which then leads to exceptional client care and agency performance.

Understanding Financials

Understanding department and agency financials is a key element to being a successful human services leader. Aside from ensuring that clients get the best services possible, many leaders are not concerned with financial aspects surrounding the operation of their department and agency. Finances drive the ability to provide services. Human service managers often assume that the Executive Director or the fundraising department address the financial need of the agency. In order to be an effective leader, or if you are aspiring to be one, you need to have a firm grasp on the financial picture of your department and agency.

The main aspects that you need to be knowledgeable about regarding financials:

- Be knowledgeable of what is fiscally involved for your department(s) to operate. This includes what is paid out monthly in salaries and benefits. This will allow you to have a good grasp on the financial picture of your department and be mindful of the revenue needed to keep your program financially vital.
- Know what your monthly budgeted revenue is (this is what your agency has budgeted for your department to do on a monthly basis to at least be financially viable).
- Ensure that your budgeted revenue is aligned with your contracted revenue. Review and have thorough knowledge of your contract(s) so you do not lose out on revenue opportunities (i.e. revenue incentives).

- Review monthly financials to verify expenditures and revenue. If any discrepancies are noted, investigate them so they can be resolved.
- Understand that some expenses (i.e. general expenses, workman's compensation, salaries for individuals who work in more than one program, or audit fees) are spread across all of the departments and need to be factored into your budget.
- If, at any period of time, you see that your department revenue is down, research the cause of decreased revenue and proactively come up with an action plan on how to address it (i.e. increase productivity, increase marketing for the program, etc.).
- Spend time with your finance department so that you can improve your knowledge of any pertinent fiscal issues.

Fiscal awareness of organizational revenue and expenses will result in financial vitality.

Facilitate a Positive Working Relationship with your Supervisor

Having a good relationship with your supervisor is just another aspect to being successful as a human services leader. Even though other concepts may garner more attention, having a productive working relationship with your supervisor will be key to you excelling in your position. While every supervisor looks for different skills and competencies from their supervisees, we have included the basics that every supervisor looks for.

Important aspects to facilitating a positive working relationship with your supervisor include:

- Be on time for all meetings and appointments. Being punctual shows your commitment and attention to detail.
- Complete assignments and tasks early if possible. This will demonstrate to your supervisor your commitment and initiative.
- Follow through and deliver. Consistently demonstrate your ability to follow through on tasks as well as the ability to produce positive outcomes.
- Offer ideas to improve existing systems. Do not be afraid to offer ideas on how to improve existing systems. Even if your idea is not implemented, it demonstrates your commitment to continuous quality improvement.
- Be proactive when faced with situations in your department. When situations arise, present a possible solution to your supervisor as opposed to waiting for them to give you direction.

- For example, if you become aware of a potential high profile situation (i.e. abuse occurring in a foster home, client at high risk for suicide, etc.) inform your supervisor of the issue and how it could be addressed proactively versus becoming a crisis situation.
- Be loyal. Even if you have differences with your supervisor do not talk negatively about them to anyone. If you do, this will at some point get back to your supervisor of what you said and will affect your relationship. This also provides the perception within the agency that you are trustworthy, focused on your job and not agency politics.
- When having supervision, have a standard list that you prepare with pertinent department information that you can cover (i.e. department revenue, staff issues, staff/client successes, human resource issues, barrier/challenges, etc.). This will assist in making supervision more organized and allow you and your supervisor to cover issues more efficiently. Include any questions that you want to go over as well so you do not forget to cover them during supervision and provide a copy to your supervisor.
- Keep your supervisor informed of all issues. Supervisors do not like surprises. As such, keep your supervisor informed of all pertinent issues occurring in your department. Give them as much notice as possible if issues arise (i.e. the department is not going to meet its revenue for the month, required clients to be seen each month was not made, human resource issues, etc.). It is always best that your supervisor finds out information from you rather than someone else.
- Ask for feedback. Be consistent in asking your supervisor for feedback on your performance. Show that you are eager for feedback as well as opportunities for improvement. With that being said, be sure that you are ready for any criticism and are open (both verbally and nonverbally). Growth can be frustrating at times, but long-term growth comes from effective feedback and opportunities to operate outside of your comfort zone.

- Ask for growth opportunities or "stretch exercises." Once you become fully acclimated with your position and you are doing well, ask your supervisor for assignments that will challenge you and allow you to learn new skills. Examples of stretch exercises include: helping to write a grant, assisting with preparing a budget, etc. Again, this shows your willingness to take on new challenges and grow.

- Do not be afraid to disagree with your supervisor. This is an area that you must tread lightly, depending on the personality of your supervisor. New supervisors, especially, tend to follow through on all directives from their supervisor even if they disagree with them. It is acceptable to disagree with your supervisor, but do so in a respectful tone. You may be surprised in the positive reaction that you may receive from your supervisor when you are able to offer alternatives and perspectives. However, always be mindful that you need to fully support whatever the final conclusion is regardless if you agree with it or not. Being in agreement with your supervisor ensures a consistent message is relayed to staff.

- Share feedback with your supervisor. If your supervisor makes a comment to you about your work that you do not agree with or understand, again, it is acceptable to discuss this with them. Also, if your supervisor acts in a way that you do not appreciate (i.e. undermining a decision that you have made), it is acceptable to respectfully bring this to their attention. Once again, be sure to be respectful when speaking to your supervisor. This is consistent with your approach with your staff in that you want them to provide you with feedback. Be judicious in your approach to providing feedback to your supervisor, as some are more receptive than others.

- Correct word choice is very important when interacting with your supervisor. Engaging in a diplomatic style that allows you to voice feedback, ideas, or concerns will allow for the best possible result. For instance, if you feel that your supervisor should go in a different direction with a decision, a few examples of diplomatic word choice include:

- "Have we thought about...."
- "We may want to consider..."
- "Another area to explore may be..."

Having a strong, positive, and open relationship with your supervisor will enhance your growth and development.

Managing Change

Change is one of the few constants within the field. Due to the human services field continually evolving, organizations have to make changes to stay current or ahead of trends. Changes can range from forms having to be revised to a new Executive Director starting with the agency. Supervisors that can successfully manage change in their departments stand to achieve higher levels of productivity, morale and client care.

Examples of change:
- Forms are revised (i.e. home visit form, progress notes, etc.)
- New responsibilities are given to employees
- A new database is used or an existing one changed
- New information needs to be tracked
- An employee leaves the department (whether by choice or has been terminated) requiring existing employees to take on added responsibilities
- A new supervisor or director has started with the agency requiring employees to re-prove themselves
- The agency changes to performance based contracts (i.e. employees have to track their billable service hours each week)

Effectively managing change:
- In situations where you are aware of changes that are going to take place, (e.g. new responsibilities for employees, reorganization, etc.) ensure that you provide employees with as much notice as possible. Employees need advanced notice

to prepare for changes in their daily routines as well as time to mentally adjust for new roles and responsibilities.

- Be mindful that the pace of change is carefully measured. There are times when supervisors or the management team may institute too many changes at once and this can quickly overwhelm employees or decrease morale.
- Ensure that changes are thoroughly explained to staff. When supervisors fail to message changes in the right way, this can lead to confusion, decreased performance, and inconsistent client care.
- Once changes have taken effect, check in with staff periodically. Having formal and informal discussions regarding their adjustment to the changes can provide you with vital information and feedback. Additionally, it provides staff an opportunity to see you and the management team as being available.
- When possible, involve staff in the change process. There are times when this is possible (i.e. changing a form) while other times it may not be.
- Do not hesitate to modify the changes that have been made based on the feedback that you have received from your staff. There are times when changes have not been carefully planned out and the feedback obtained from employees confirms this. Recognize the helpful feedback and make the necessary adjustments.
- When an employee has left the department this can be a very difficult process to manage. If the employee has been terminated you will have to engage in damage control, as staff may be quick to blame you or the management team for their dismissal. Moreover, whenever an employee leaves, existing staff have to take on extra work to cover. This can cause increased stress for the department, so be mindful how work is spread out and offer to take on extra work as appropriate (i.e. covering home visits, making phone calls, filing, etc.).

Effective supervisors recognize that change is constant, continuous, and are prepared.

Focus on Continuous Quality Improvement

Avoid the trap of the status quo. Too often, the same ineffective systems are being used because "that is the way we have always done things." Be innovative and on the lookout for ways to improve service delivery or enhance existing systems to make them more efficient. Having an innovative approach will ensure continuous quality improvement toward optimal client care.

Ensure that your department is running as efficiently as possible through:

- Many organizations have a shared or "groups" drive that can be accessed by anyone in the department. Ensure that all client records are organized and stored on the groups drive; it enables quick access in case a staff member who is working with the client is out. Moreover, create folders for contact information, training information, etc., that is readily accessible by all employees.
- Ask for a peer on your level to review the organizational processes that you have in place in your department and ask for their feedback in how to become more efficient.
- Conduct client satisfaction surveys. Making random calls to verify how staff is performing and how clients are receiving services will assist in evaluating how client needs are being met. Data from these two processes provides indications on how to improve service delivery for your department. Additionally, this provides you with direct feedback of how your

staff is interacting and helping clients, and can be used in their evaluation.

- Continually check that files are up to date and have the necessary information contained in them. As a supervisor, be sure to conduct random file reviews on a regular basis. You should never have to "get ready" for an audit, as your files should always be up to date and ready to be reviewed at any given time. Develop a tracking system to demonstrate what files you have reviewed and when they were reviewed so that you review all client charts within a specific period of time (i.e. three months).

- Be innovative with your staff by having your monthly team meeting outside of the workplace, plan a half day "retreat" outside of the office to work on team building exercises, etc. Any unique ways to look at quality improvement will go a long way toward building an innovative department and agency.

- Provide the environment for staff to come up with ideas to improve existing systems or develop new systems to make the department run more efficiently (i.e. use of a suggestion box). Consider providing recognition or rewards for improving existing systems or developing new ones (i.e. a $20 gas card, gift card to a restaurant, time off, etc.). Staff should feel encouraged to share innovative ideas.

- Reach out to other agencies and form relationships with personnel who provide the same or similar services as your department and/or agency. This will assist you in finding out what their tracking systems are, curriculums that they use with clients, billing systems, etc. You may be able to share ideas and help each other problem-solve issues that arise in your agency or community.

- Look into systems like Lean Six Sigma to assist your group or department with improving existing processes or devising new ones to increase efficiency and organization. While initially utilized in manufacturing, it has become increasingly popular in service industries. Lean Six Sigma helps to create an environment of continuous quality improvement through different levels of employee expertise and projects aimed at increasing staff productivity, employee retention, etc.

- Obtain feedback from external stakeholders in the community regarding the performance of your agency, department and staff. Use surveys such as www.surveymonkey.com, paper surveys, or ask questions. This feedback will be helpful to see how the community perceives you and the services that you are providing. Remember, perception is often reality.
- Always be on the lookout for ways to improve department performance. Additionally, encourage employees to have the same approach, and champion ideas and efforts to improve existing systems. Even if a suggestion is not utilized, staff that buy in to the value of improvement are more productive.

Always be committed to improving your own performance:

- When meeting with your supervisor, always ask for constructive feedback on your performance and pointers on how you can improve. Be receptive to the feedback that you receive, regardless of your initial response to the information.
- Your constant commitment to improvement by asking for feedback shows your supervisor that you are focused on continuous improvement and growth.
- Find books and journal articles that will expand your knowledge on particular treatment modalities, knowledge in your particular field, or management skills.
- Be conscious in observing other supervisors, peers, etc., regarding their overall approach and adopt those behaviors into your repertoire.

Addressing continuous quality improvement demonstrates that you are conscientious and committed to having high quality standards for yourself and the agency.

Problem Solving and Risk Management from a Global Perspective

Human service leaders constantly come across situations that require excellent problem solving and risk management skills. How you approach and solve situations is important in how you will be perceived as a successful leader in your organization and within your community. Successful problem solving skills include, but are not limited to: seeing a situation from a 360-degree perspective (i.e. from the perspective of all participants involved), incorporating risk management into every decision (i.e. assessing the potential safety issues related to any decision), and approaching situations from a global standpoint (i.e. how will this affect the agency or what global factors may impact this decision?).

The perspective of effective problem solving and risk management also relates to external stakeholders (i.e. funders, other community agencies, etc.). Working in collaboration in problem solving situations with external partners helps to address larger, systemic issues that affect all clients in the community. By effectively collaborating with external stakeholders, the effects of territorialism can be reduced by looking at a solution from a global standpoint. This seeks to promote a win-win scenario for everyone involved, which only helps to improve client care.

A key aspect to effectively problem solving issues is the ability to see the global picture. By seeing the global picture, one is able to not only look at the immediate issues surrounding a given situation, but they can see how their decision will impact the agency as a whole. The ability to see situations from a global viewpoint takes time to develop, as many new supervisors struggle to see beyond the scope of the issue they are dealing with. This is a skill that is valuable for all employees to learn as well, as it will improve their ability to understand why certain organizational decisions are made.

Important points to consider in effectively problem solving situations from a global perspective:

- Balance employee time off versus department and agency need: consistent coverage to meet client needs is always a priority. Oftentimes it is difficult for employees to see how their individual needs affect total client care. For example, if an employee requests time off when another colleague is already out and coverage is already limited, it is important to inform the employee why you were not able to approve their time off.
- Incorporate additional individual and department responsibilities when directed by funders or senior management. How you, as a human services leader, message these additional responsibilities to your staff to accept and implement them is essential to managing change in the field. It is important that you are able to deliver the message that additional responsibilities have been added without your staff feeling like they are being "dumped" on. This is a common feeling that staff has, but it is your role to relay this difficult message so department morale is not adversely affected.
  - When situations like this arise, try to brainstorm ways for the extra work to be equally divided or for the team to look at how existing systems can be streamlined to make the transition easier.
- Understand the importance of problem solving long-term, systemic issues versus "putting out fires" to address immediate situations. Many times it is easier to address the current issue without addressing the larger issue at hand. This may involve having to put together a task force with other agencies to address community issues so that specific problems do not

continue to arise. Similarly, this may involve putting together an internal task force to address agency issues which impact client care, employee development, etc.

- Be mindful of the related liability potential in regards to decisions and actions. Expertise in this area is limited for most, so consultation is important. Examples in which risk management principles apply include: assessing lethality risk for a client, assessing environmental safety issues for staff, transportation of clients, release of information and consent issues for client care, etc. These all impact risk management decisions for an agency. Effective human service leaders can look at a situation and assess and evaluate it from several perspectives, not just one.

- When addressing issues with external stakeholders, be willing to acknowledge other perspectives as well as mediate a compromise in relation to coming up with the best solution to an issue (For example, if an issue arises with a community provider and differences of opinion persist, take time to clarify the points that are causing the conflicts. Use language such as, "I am a little unclear as to your point of view, can you clarify this for me?" This can help to diffuse the conflict that is occurring by focusing on the true issue at hand.).

- Pride yourself in having a positive and collaborative relationship with community providers. Your ability to be seen as competent, trustworthy, and an effective problem-solver by the community results in any interaction that you have with external stakeholders. This will also promote and enhance collaboration with key stakeholders in the community. Moreover, this will help you in being seen as an effective problem-solver within your agency and in the community.

Viewing situations with a global perspective enhances problem solving and risk managment skills.

About the Authors

Tim Nolan, M.S., M.S., has worked in the human sevices field for approvimately 10 years and currently works as an Assistant Director at a community based care agency in Broward County, Florida. He is also a faculty memeber with the University of Phoenix, where he teaches various courses in the human services. Tim earned his master's degrees from Capella University and Carlos Albizu Unviersity. Tim resides in North Lauderdale, Florida with his wife, Elaine.

Keith Johnson, M.S. has worked in the human service field for approximately 20 years and is currently a Director of Community Based Programs for a child welfare organization in Palm Beach County, Florida. He also works as a therapist part-time. He earned his master's degree from Nova University. Keith resides in Boynton Beach, Florida with his wife Carolyn.

The authors are available for leadership trainings on a variety of topics and can be reached via email at: tim@humanservices leadership.org.

CPSIA information can be obtained at www.ICGtesting.com
Printed in the USA
LVOW05s1929070214

372847LV00007B/85/P